MYSTICS AND SCHOLARS

The Calgary Conference on Mysticism 1976

edited by

HAROLD COWARD
and
TERENCE PENELHUM

SUPPLEMENTS / 3

KANSAS SCHOOL OF RELIGION
UNIVERSITY OF KANSAS
1300 OREAD AVENUE
?ENCE KANSAS 66044

MYSTICS AND SCHOLARS

Edited By

Harold Coward and Terence Penelhum

Canadian Cataloguing in Publication Data

Calgary Conference on Mysticism, 1976.
  Mystics and scholars

(SR supplements ; 3)

Bibliography: p.
Includes index.
ISBN 0-919812-04-X pa.

1. Mysticism - Congresses. I. Coward, Harold, 1936-
II. Penelhum, Terence, 1929-   III. Title.
IV. Series.

BL625.C35 1976   291.4'2   C77-001127-6

TABLE OF CONTENTS

ABOUT THE AUTHORS

Joseph Epes Brown is Professor of Religious Studies at the University of Montana. He is a graduate of the University of Stockholm. His published books include *The Spiritual Legacy of the American Indian* and *The Sacred Pipe*.

Harold Coward is Assistant Professor and Head of Religious Studies at the University of Calgary. He is a graduate of the University of Alberta and McMaster University, and has been a Visiting Research Scholar at Banaras Hindu University. He is the author of *Bhartṛhari*.

Herbert Guenther is Professor and Head of the Department of Far Eastern Studies at the University of Saskatchewan. He studied in Munich, Vienna, India, and Tibet and has taught at Vienna University, Lucknow University, the Sanskrit University, and the International School of America before assuming his position at the University of Saskatchewan. His many books include *Das Seelenproblem im alteren Buddhismus*, *Yuganaddha - The Tantric Way of Life*, *Tibetan Buddhism without Mystification*, *Buddhist Philosophy in Theory and Practice*, and *Kindly Bent to East Us I*, *II* and *III*.

John Heintz is Professor and Head of the Department of Philosophy at the University of Calgary and is a graduate of Duke University. He is the author of *Subjects and Predicables: A Study in Subject-Predicate Asymmetry*.

John Hick is H.G. Wood Professor of Theology at the University of Birmingham. He is a graduate of the Universities of Edinburgh, Oxford, and Cambridge, and has taught at Cornell, Princeton, and Cambridge. His many writings include *Faith and Knowledge*, *Evil and the God of Love*, *Christianity at the Centre*, *God and Universe of Faiths*, and *Death and Eternal Life*.

Terence Penelhum is Professor of Philosophy and Religious Studies at the University of Calgary, and is a graduate of Edinburgh and Oxford. He has written *Survival and Disembodied Exist-*

ence, Religion and Rationality, and *Hume.*

Swami Prabuddhananda is Minister of the Vedanta Society of
Northern California at San Francisco. He is a monk of the
Ramakrishna order of India.

Walter H. Principe, c.s.b. is Professor of History of Christian
Thought at the Pontifical Institute of Mediaeval Studies, the
University of St. Michael's College, and the Graduate Centre
for Mediaeval Studies and the Graduate Centre for Religious
Studies at the University of Toronto. He is a graduate of
the École des Hautes Études at Paris and the Pontifical
Institute of Mediaeval Studies at Toronto. He is the author
of four volumes on *The Theology of the Hypostatic Union in
the Early Thirteenth Century.*

Rabbi Zalman Schachter is Professor of Religion, Temple University. He graduated from the Hebrew Union College. In past
years he has guided congregations in New England and previously taught at the University of Manitoba. He is the author
of *Fragments of a Future Scroll: Hasidism for the Aquarian
Age.*

Eido Shimano is Roshi and Abbot of International Dai Bosatsu
Zendo, New York. He is also the President of the Zen Studies
Society, New York. He was born and trained in Japan. He is
co-author of *Namudaibosa* and has published several transla-
tions of Buddhist works.

Ninian Smart is Professor of Religious Studies at the University
of Lancaster, England, and of Religious Studies at the University of California, Santa Barbara. He has served in British Intelligence and is author of *Doctrine and Argument in
Indian Philosophy, The Yogi and the Devotee* and other works.

Brother David Steindl-Rast graduated from the University of Vienna
and has been a Post-Doctoral Fellow at Cornell University.
He is a member of the Benedictine Monastery of Mount Saviour,
Pine City, New York. He is co-founder of the Center for
Spiritual Studies and has contributed to many books and
periodicals.

PREFACE

In September of 1976 a group of some fifty scholars and practising mystics gathered at the University of Calgary. The chief objective of the Conference was to ponder and assess the nature of mysticism in its Eastern, Western and North American Indian forms. The method the Conference followed was somewhat unusual in that it aimed at a dialogue between the practising mystics and the scholars.

After Professor Principe's general introduction to "Mysticism: Its Meaning and Varieties" the practising mystics each spoke about their own personal experience. Then it was the scholars' turn to analyze the data of personal experience presented by the mystics. This was the first formal step in the dialogue. It was immediately followed by the second formal step -- a response from the mystics: Did the scholar in his presentation understand the data of the mystics' personal experiences? Was the scholarly analysis perceptive or did it miss the point? By following this format in the order of speakers, i.e., mystic, scholar, mystic, scholar, the Conference formally established the desired dialogue: the scholar attempting to be true to the data of personal experience presented by the mystic; the mystic, in response, acting as a check on the academic interpretation offered by the scholar. Of course, once established by the Conference speakers, the dialogue continued in the discussion sessions following each presentation.

What this book presents to the reader is not the outcome of the dialogue, but the personal statements and papers from which the dialogue began. Of course there is a degree to which the dialogue is already present, in that the papers of the scholars were written with the statements of the mystics in hand. Among some of the philosophers present, a set of more formal comments on each others presentations was recorded and these have been included.

A special word needs to be added about one of the practising mystics whose comments do not appear in this book. Rufus Goodstriker, of the Blood Indians, Cardston, Alberta, spoke on behalf of the North American Indian Tradition. In that tradition, it is held that the sacred teachings and practices must not be written down. They are only to be transmitted by the spoken word of the one who holds them sacred. The editors have respected the wishes of Rufus Goodstriker, and the teachings of his tradition. None of his words are reproduced in this volume although references to his statements appear from time to time in some of the papers. A good idea of the approach of the Native American Indian tradition can be gained from Joseph Epes Brown's paper.

This Conference was made possible by the financial support of

PREFACE

the Canada Council and the University of Calgary, for which we
are grateful.

Harold Coward

Terence Penelhum

December 1, 1976

Department of Religious Studies
University of Calgary
Calgary, Alberta, Canada

Mysticism: Its Meaning and Varieties
By WALTER H. PRINCIPE

Back in 1960 the humorous popular poet, Ogden Nash, began his
'Laments for a Dying Language' with these words:
  What's the monster of this week?
  "Mystique" ---
  A noun that in its current arcane use leaves me frigid,
  Since it is not to be found in either the O.E.D. or *Webster's
  Unabridged*.[1]
The poet may have muted his plaint in the following year when
'mystique'[2] found its way into a new edition of Webster's Unabridged;[2] but such modification of language, whether by newly-
coined words or rapid change in meaning of older words, does
point up one problem facing our seminar on mysticism, a word with
the same root as the one abhorred by Ogden Nash. Unlike 'mystique',
the word 'mysticism' has long been found in the *Oxford English
Dictionary* and in *Webster's Unabridged* and *Abridged*, but the general carefree attitude about language that caused Nash's laments
has afflicted this word and, therefore, the notions people have
about it. So, as you wander through a bookstore you are liable
to see a section-heading such as 'occultism and mysticism': in
fact, one Toronto bookstore simply titles the section 'occultism'
and puts under it the books on mysticism! Again, a respectable
editor's cover blurb about a serious book on mysticism links it
with 'visions and occult powers'.[3] Spiritualistic seances or
practices, voices, rappings, levitations, trances or prophetic
utterances are often dubbed 'mystical'. Any kind of experience
of an 'altered state of consciousness' is immediately labeled
'mystical'; any *mysterious* experience is called 'mystical', likely
because the once-honourable word 'mystery' has been preempted for
entertaining novels or movies that are really puzzles rather than
true mysteries. All kinds of literature are described as mystical
even if they flow only from poetic intuition, nature lore, or vague
dreaminess. A newspaper columnist, noting that the Olympic games
are held 'every fourth year after the first full moon at the
height of the summer', suggested recently that 'lunacy could be
associated in some mystical way with the choice of the date'.[4]
And last May the *Toronto Star's* headline-writer announced:
'Scientist offers electronic way to mysticism' -- this to entice
readers to an article about a 'meditation machine' or revolving
bed that is 'intended', says the photo-caption, 'to help people
enjoy the spiritual experiences formerly available only to religious mystics'.[5]
  Well, to lament this imprecision is likely futile. Yet the
important seminar on mysticism that we begin this evening should

1

at least try to reach some precision about the very subject we
shall be discussing. My purpose will be to try to sort out some
positive description of mysticism that may help to focus the seminar discussions and thereby eliminate distracting side-issues,
especially certain experiences that are sometimes linked or i-
dentified with mysticism. I have also been asked to say something
about the varieties of mysticism. In doing so in the latter part
of my paper, I shall not attempt the impossible task of trying
to describe the manifold teachings or accounts of mystical experience found in different traditions (that will be in part the
work of others in the seminar); rather, I shall try to show the
sort of questions asked about mysticism and answered differently by different mystics. This difference in answers will, I think
indicate some of the variety found amoung mystics and mystical
traditions.

It is not my task, I should add, to discuss such crucial problems as the methodologies to be used in studying mysticism; the
criteria for judging mystical experiences; variations in preparatory techniques such as yoga or meditation or use of mantras or
mandalas or images; the place of meditation on scriptures or su-
tras or on the life of the great religious figures; kabbalistic
techniques of combining and meditating on Hebrew letters or symbols of God. These matters will likely come to the fore in the
seminar discussions.

Let us, then, first of all try to find a more specific meaning
of 'mysticism' and 'mystical' that can serve as focus for our
discussions. A few remarks about the origin of the word itself
might help us. 'Mysticism' and its cognate 'mystical' come from
the Greek and so are part of our Greco-Roman cultural tradition,
but they are applied by specialists in religious studies to such
experiences in other traditions: these, of course have their own
terms, whether it be samadhi, satori, nirvana or sunyata,
devekuth, fana, or shimpi.

The Greek word at the root of our English words 'mysticism' and
'mystical' is the verb *muein*, which means 'to close the eyes'[6].
At first among the Greeks 'mystical' referred to rites or ceremonies of mystery cults that were hidden or closed to the eyes
of all but initiates. The word came, however, to take on a common-
place use referring to the hidden or mysterious, and it was this
common-place and even secular use that early Christian writers
adopted. They applied the term 'mystical' to the Christian mystery, the mystery of Christ as first experienced in the bible,
then in the liturgy, and finally in a person's spiritual life.
(One should note at once the close link between 'mystical' and
'mystery'. Both words derive from the same Greek root: *muein*.)
With respect to the bible, patristic authors such as Clement of
Alexandria, Origen, and Didymus interpreted the whole bible with
reference to Christ and his mystery and spoke of this as a

'mystical interpretation' or as finding the 'mystical meaning'
of the sacred texts. (Among Jewish mystics, the kabbala also
seeks a deeper mystical meaning in the Hebrew scriptures, this
in relation to the mystery of God and creation.) Regarding the
liturgy, Christian authors applied 'mystical' especially to the
Eucharist to refer to its hidden reality, the reality veiled or
hidden in the consecrated bread and wine, that is, the mystery of
Christ. Thus the Fathers spoke of the Eucharist as a 'mystical
food', a 'mystical banquet' and as 'the mystical body of Christ'.
the body of Christ in mystery.

From these meanings came the third, the one closest to our topic:
they used 'mystical' for a deeper spiritual experience, that is,
direct experiential knowledge of God by a person plunging into the
mystical meaning of the bible, sharing in the mystery of Christ
in the liturgy, especially in Baptism and in the Eucharist, and
thereby being transported into the mystical realities, the
'mystical cloud of unknowing' that Moses had entered on Mount
Sinai when he conversed with God. In one sense every believer
was considered a mystic in that he plunged into this mystery
through the bible and the liturgy, but very early the term was
used more of those who experienced deeper and more frequent entry
into this world whether in the liturgy or in personal reflection
and prayer.

This doctrine of the Greek patristic authors flowed, together
with important neo-Platonic elements from Plotinus and Proclus,
into Pseudo-Dionysius the Areopagite, an enigmatic author of the
late fifth or early sixth century. His four major works include
one called *Mystical Theology*, which describes the spiritual ascent
to God by negation of positive ideas or concepts in a manner not
unlike the emptying or voiding prescribed by some Eastern traditions (his other works, however, speak of the importance of love,
and of the role of Christ and the liturgy -- themes of his too
often neglected by scholars). Because the Pseudo-Dionysius
successfully passed himself off as a disciple of the Apostle Paul,
his writings influenced the Christian West enormously. Although
all three meanings of 'mystical' can be found in his writings,
it was the third, experiential knowledge of the hidden mystery
of God, that most caught the attention of medieval Christian
mystics and authors and thereby fixed the term and concept for
subsequent centuries down to our time. (We might note here that
some today find the term 'mysticism' less satisfactory than others
such as 'contemplation' or 'illumination' or 'theopathy'. But
others, at least some Christian scholars, prefer 'mysticism' for
its link with 'mystery' which associates it with Christ and the
community.)

Leaving this rapid survey of the use of the word, can we find a
fairly determined meaning for the reality itself of mysticism
or mystical experience? In trying to decide among various

claimants, one might well be accused of a dogmatism like Humpty
Dumpty's in *Through the Looking-Glass* when he said to Alice:
'When *I* use a word, it means just what I choose it to mean --
neither more nor less.' What we can say here is that pragmati-
cally and concretely the organizers of this seminar and most if
not all of the participants wish to focus on mysticism or mystical experience as described in one way or another in all the
great spiritual traditions, that is, a relatively rare but universal and liberating experience either of self-oblivion or
nirvana as in Buddhism or of a special relationship with the
Deity, whether this remain unnamed or be named as God, the
Absolute, the Ultimate Reality, the All-Holy and Almighty, Cosmic
Reality, the Ground of Being, the Transcendent or the One. (I
shall use some of these terms rather interchangeably, realizing
that there are individual preferences and that some would prefer no such term at all.)

What does mystical experience include? It is difficult to find
a description, let alone a definition, that would cover every
mystical experience such as they are described by mystics of
differing traditions. For example, the mystical experience of
nirvana or sunyata within certain forms of Buddhism seems to set
it apart from others. Yet even this, I think, could be included
in a very broad description if we say that mystical experience
is an intuitional or experiential knowledge beyond sense knowledge, beyond reasoning, beyond poetic or artistic intuition; an
experiential or intuitional knowledge that is passive, transi-
tory, far less permanent than sense knowledge or reasoning; an
experience that is, finally, inexpressible.[7] Perhaps saying even
this is too much for some forms of Buddhist mystical doctrine
(whatever the concrete experience may be) because in some forms
of Buddhism it seems that even knowledge or consciousness is held
to disappear as the self is dissolved or absorbed in nirvana or
attains emptiness or the void: there may be no point in speaking of knowledge, passivity, transiency, or inexpressibility in
such a state or non-state.

In most mystical traditions, however, including some Buddhist
ones, certain other elements commonly enter into the mystical
experience, chief among them being the experience of love related
to a divine Being or Ultimate Reality. Thus one might add to the
previous very general description those other elements that would
not fit all traditions but that would be accepted by most, among
them many Hindus, and generally the Jewish, Christian and Muslim
traditions. In these traditions mystical experience is a loving
experiential knowledge or consciousness of God or the Absolute
or the Transcendent; of God experienced as present awesomely, yet
benevolently and lovingly, and as closely united with oneself;
a loving experiential knowledge of God or Ultimate Reality in
which the human person remains passive and receptive within the

active giving and penetrating presence, and in which the more
profound the experience, the less is the person focused on himself,
or herself, the more is he or she totally absorbed in the Awesome
Lover experienced as present; an experience in which conceptual
knowledge fades away, even if imagination is not always stilled,
and in which direct intuitive awareness is dominant.

Its immediate effects in the person are often, and simultaneously,(1) fear before awesomeness, before mystery, before the
call to self-surrender and self-transcendence; (2) intense joy
and consummate happiness at the experience of being loved so
powerfully; (3) almost complete or perhaps complete loss of the
sense of self for a time as, for example, in ecstatic rapture,
although ecstatic rapture is not the only or the essential trait
of mystical experience; (4) a sense of being emptied or pene-
trated, or of being 'dug out' or of being cleansed or purified,
sometimes as if by fire.

Following upon this experience the person generally has a sense
of wonder and peace and harmony and joy that overflows into a
spirit of communion with and benevolence towards other persons
and all other things -- animals, plants, the earth, the whole of
created reality -- because all these are seen as also loved by
God and because God is experienced as present in all persons and
things. Praise of God in Himself and in his creatures arises
spontaneously. Another effect is often a kind of tension in the
mystic between a desire for solitude to be with the Beloved and
a desire to serve those in whom the Beloved is found and who are
loved by the Beloved.

Let us review some of these last characteristics briefly. First
the mystic discovers God or Ultimate Reality as the Reality that
is the ultimate mystery beyond all things and not just one being
or reality among others. Second, the knowledge involved in this
discovery is beyond sense, imagination, poetic or artistic intuition, or reasoning: it is an experiential and seemingly direct if still obscure knowledge, a higher intuition that seems
unmediated and beyond any other human experience. Third, God
is experienced as immanent, as interior to the deepest realms of
one's being, as giving and bestowing, and the human subject
feels called to be more and more passive, receptive, totally
self-forgetful. Fourth, this receptivity involves both an ineffable knowledge and an experience of being loved, both so over-
powering as to be awesome and even dreadful. Both Abraham
Abulafia and Teresa of Avila said that the experience of ecstatic
rapture is, at the start, as frightful as if one were about to
die. Fifth, the mystic experiences a surge of new power of being
and activity, an increase of energy, an enlarged awareness, a
changed outlook on values and desires so that everything other
than the Reality he or she has experienced seems either worth-
less or secondary, even though everything in creation is to be

5

cherished and loved in the Beloved's love for it. The mystic
experiences a call to live henceforth totally for God or the
Absolute and to serve others within and under the impulse of
this infused, loving knowledge, presence and union.

Sixth, the greatest mystics among the yogi or sufis or a
Christian like John of the Cross will insist that the experiences themselves, and whatever feelings and emotions result
from it, are nevertheless not the Ultimate Reality, not the
One to whom the person is united: they are received, human or
above-human but created experiences and must not be confused with
the One who is experienced (I think that this point is important
for distinguishing mystical experience from altered states of
consciousness produced by drugs or other purely mechanical techniques). Finally, all mystics agree that the experience cannot
be adequately described by any human language, especially by
ordinary language or scientific terminology. So they often revert
to paradox or poetry or symbolism in a failing but desperate
attempt to speak of it, unless, as many do, they prefer to feel
obliged to remain silent about it. How can one describe a rain-
bow or a sunset to a blind man? How can a lover describe his
beloved to one who has not loved his beloved as he has? How can
one describe the ineffable mystical experience to one who has not
received it? (One exception might be noted in reference to
language, that of the Kabbalists. It is not that they think
language can describe the experience: in fact, they generally
recoil from such attempts for reasons other than linguistic
ones; but their mystical tradition holds that the Hebrew language itself, because it comes from God, reaches God and has a
mystical value because it reflects the fundamental spiritual nature of the world and its relation to God.)

If the characteristics I have outlined are indeed those of
mystical experience, one can see why mystics reject other experiences put forth as mystical. Visions, for example. Although
some mystics have experienced visions and although some vision-
aries are thought to be or claim to be mystics, the spiritual
masters generally distinguish the two and refuse to equate visions with their loving intuitional experience of the ineffable or
with nirvana or samadhi. Also rejected as non-mystical are the
hearing of voices, prophetic utterances, or speaking in tongues.
Mystical experience is held to be other than the enthusiastic
intensities produced by fervent and exhausting sermons, singing,
handclapping and the like. Powers of healing or working mir-
acles are not considered mystical: in fact, one scholar of
Sufism told me that the sufi searching for mystical union is
urged to avoid them as a hindrance on his way, and John of the
Cross is equally severe against these and all the other things I
have mentioned as being hindrances to true mysticism or contemplation. Also rejected are the drug-induced wanderings of the

imagination through brilliant and highly-charged realms of
psychic adventure. The world of spiritism and of other preter-
natural or parapsychological phenomena fail to meet the criteria
of most mystics. So too does simple inspirational communing
with nature, although for those habituated to mystical experience
the beauty and harmony of nature can be the occasion for rising
to the loftier and more intense realms of experience, or the
place where their experience overflows in the way I have already
suggested.

What of Yoga exercises and the techniques of various kinds of
meditation ranging from transcendental meditation to the
Exercises of St. Ignatius? These may be excellent preparations of
the body, imagination, and mind but they are in themselves only
preparatory, closing out distractions, concentrating the person's
inner attention, and fostering an attitude of peace, openness
and receptivity. But the mystical experience is something beyond
these, and for most it is seen as gift given, not something
reached by techniques alone.

What of scientific probings into the neuro-physiological effects
of these preparatory techniques or, if it is indeed possible,
of mystical experiences themselves? Such probings are interesting and may lead to interesting insights, but I think it true to
say that for those who have had mystical experience such as I have
tried to describe it, these probings can never reach the core of
the experience. Even of the level of scientific study, Professor
D. H. Salman of the Department of Psychology of the Université de
Montréal has pointed out how inadequate it is to examine only
neuro-physiological data. He insists -- rightly, I believe --that
one must consider 'such fundamental psychological factors as
personality structure, beliefs and values, and motivations, not
to mention the dynamics of basic attitudes'.[10] As I have said,
for the mystic the heart of the experience is not his or her own
perception, not even his or her loving intuition, but the
Ultimate Reality, the Absolute that is experienced. Therefore,
just because theta-waves have been measured as coordinates of
subjects meditating deeply, it does not follow that every time
theta-waves are observed or possibly produced by training techniques or drugs or whatever there is a mystical experience involved. All dogs are animals but not all animals are dogs. All
true mystical experiences might be accompanied by theta-wave
patterns (which is still to be proved) but the existence of such
patterns fails to prove the existence of mystical experience.
All these negations may sound rather dogmatic and elitist, but
unless we wish to deny the experience of mystics, we must respect
their witness to the otherness of this experience. Those who
refuse this witness might well be in the position of the person
who asked a Muslim spiritual master: 'Who is a Sufi?' He answered. 'A Sufi does not ask who a Sufi is.'[11]

MYSTICISM: MEANING AND VARIETIES

Let us now turn away from negations to more positive statements, or rather to questions that lead to affirmations. Here
we enter upon the last topic of our paper, the varieties of
mysticism, because the answers or attitudes to these questions
bring out many varieties and emphases in mystical traditions.

One of the first questions to be asked is whether the Ultimate
Reality experienced is personal or not. Here there are divisions
among mystical traditions and within individual ones. There are
mystics of what has been called the 'I-It' view and others of the
'I-Thou' view, or Mysticism of Infinity by contracts with
Mysticism of Personality.[12] In the 'I-It' view or Mysticism of
Infinity the Ultimate Reality is conceived of as the Being beyond all being, or as Non-being or Nothing, or as the Soul of
the Universe or as Universal Mind. This form of mysticism is
found in Plotinus, the Upanishads, some forms of Kabbalism and of
Sufism, and in authors such as Blake, Huysmans, Emerson, and
Goethe (if indeed their experiences were truly mystical). For
the 'I-Thou' view or Mysticism of Personality the relation between the human subject and Ultimate Reality is experienced as
personal, that of creature to Creator, of child to Father or
Mother, or of lover and Beloved. This form of mystical experience is described in the Bhagavad-Gita and is generally to be
found among Hindu mystics of the Vaishnava and Shaivite traditions as well as among most Jewish, Christian, and Muslim mystics.

Related to this is another question we have already had to
touch upon: is the personal self or identity of the mystic maintained in this unifying experience or is the mystic's personal
self or identity absorbed and lost completely in nirvana, or in
union with the Ultimate, the One, the Universal Soul? Here again
one sees a contrast and indeed a sharp division. Often Mysti-
cisms of Infinity tend toward or assert the complete ontological
(and not only psychological-empirical) absorption of the personal
self in the One or the All: the famous phrase of the Upanishad:
Tat tvam asi ('Thou art that') expresses this, and Buddhists insist that the self is one of the delusions that must be elim-
inated for escape from Karma and reincarnation and for entry into
nirvana. Although some mystics of the 'I-Thou' view or Mysticism
of Personality have spoken of complete personal identification
with God or at least have been interpreted as teaching it, most
have held that the human person's identity is maintained even
within most intensive union with the Person of God: Jewish and
Christian mystics have been perhaps the most insistent upon this.

A third question also evokes variation in reply or emphasis.
In the very mystical experience as opposed to the preparatory
phases, what relation, if any, is there between knowledge and love:
are both present and intermingled or is there only experiential
knowledge without love or experiential love without knowledge?
The love-aspect seems almost or completely lacking in some forms

8

of Hindu mysticism, for example, that of Shankara,[13] in most
forms of Buddhist mysticism, and in Merkabah mysticism in the
Jewish tradition. But most mystics in other traditions speak of
a fusion of experiential knowledge and love. Even here, however,
some mystics lay more stress on contemplative knowledge or illumination or gnosis or theosophy while others emphasize union with
God or the All-Holy through love: thus Ramanuja and Ramakrishna
among Hindus stressed bhakti or loving devotion: in the kabbalistic mystical tradition, kabbalism tends to be somewhat more
theosophical and knowledge- oriented than hasidism, a tradition
emphasizing piety and love rather more than knowledge; among
Christian mystics, although none denies the role of love in
mystical union, one finds greater emphasis on illumination and
knowledge in the Pseudo-Dionysius or in Eckhart, and more emphasis on love in mystics like Bernard of Clairvaux, Francis of
Assisi, Teresa of Avila, or John of the Cross.

A fourth question: what is the role of personal effort and what
element of gift is involved in mystical experience? In some
mystical traditions the main and at times unique stress is on
personal effort, personal preparation, with no reliance on outside aid except perhaps that of a master or guru to instruct:
this tendency is found more, as one might expect, among the
I-It mystics or among those such as Buddhists for whom there is no
distinction between I and It, let alone between I and Thou.
Many other traditions, however, hold that an element of gift or
grace is absolutely essential. All traditions would insist on the
absolute need of preparatory efforts -- withdrawal of some kind,
concentration, preparatory asceticism. Growth toward mystical
experience is generally seen as progress from a stage of purga-
tion or purification through a stage of illumination or contemplation (where mystical experience begins) to a stage of union.
For some, illumination and absorption in the void or the One is
the ultimate; for others the ultimate is a close union of persons
in love that is often expressed by using human analogies such as
spiritual betrothal or spiritual marriage.

Among those who see the need for a divine gift and call there
arises a subsidiary question: is this gift open to all, a possible and normal development of a dedicated life of service and
prayer under grace? Or is it a matter of divine free choice of a
select few, something extraordinary and unrelated to previous
growth in spirituality? This question has received different
answers. All traditions have exceptionally gifted mystics and
teachers, but does this rule out mystical experience of a less
outstanding yet real type? One example of this debate occurred
among Roman Catholics earlier in this century. The older
Catholic tradition seemed to hold mystical experience as open to
all who genuinely abandoned themselves to God and cooperated
fully with His gracious activity in them. But in recent centuries,

because of the excesses of the Quietists, mysticism came to be
viewed by some with suspicion (as it was in most Protestant traditions but for different reasons); mysticism was seen as something extraordinary and not to be sought by ordinary Christians.
In recent years the debate I mentioned seems to have subsided in
favour of a rather general acceptance of mystical experience as a
normal if not statistically numerous development of the life of
grace and prayer, something one can hope and prepare for by self-
renunciation and fidelity to a life of love and prayer. Other
mystical traditions have also experienced such alternations between an elitist view and a more universalist view.

A fifth question: what is the attitude of the different mystical traditions or of individual mystics to the body, the emotions, and intellectual thought? All mystics agree on the need
for discipline in use of the body, the emotions, the imagination,
and intellectual thought. Yet there are differences in attitude.
Some, and I think this could be said of many Eastern traditions,
view these as sources of hindrance and delusion, as evils to be
escaped. Others view them as good though needing discipline, and
as open to harmony and integration with a higher life, a harmony
and integration that is most perfectly achieved through mystical
experience. Different attitudes here give rise to divergencies
regarding human activity in general and asceticism in particular.
For example, Professor Zalman Schachter points out that some
'fundamentalist' kabbalists are wary of the body and carnality,
whereas 'humanist' kabbalists seek to integrate the body and
carnality within spirituality.[14] In Christian mysticism
Manichean and Stoic strains often led to mistrust of the body
and emotions and sometimes to excessive and competitive ascetic
feats, whereas Thomas Aquinas (who was a mystic and theologian of
mystical contemplation among other things) viewed the body, the
emotions, imagination and intellect as good: for him the work of
virtuous activity is to order all these, especially through love,
so that the person is disposed for mystical contemplation.

A sixth question concerns the relation of mysticism to religion
-- to religious bodies of believers or churches, to religious
worship, liturgy, indeed to belief itself and the life of organized religion. In some cases, as in early Buddhism, there seems
to have been a total split, even a rejection of religion or belief, but later Buddhism, especially the Mahayana tradition,
developed extensive religious doctrines and practices. In other
cases, as in some Jewish, Christian, or Muslim instances, there
has sometimes been tension between the individual mystic or group
of mystics and the religious body to which they belong. In most
cases, however, mystics have seen themselves as solidly anchored
within their religious communities and traditions and view their
experiences as part of the fruits of their religious tradition
and often as given for reinvigorating these traditions. As

Gershom Scholem says, 'History shows that the great mystics were faithful adherents of the great religions.'[15]

In line with this comes another question: what is the relation between mysticism and the great religious and mystical leaders such as the Buddha, Moses, Jesus Christ, Mohammed, Ramanuja, Ramakrishna, etc.? Are they important primarily or exclusively for their teaching and example, or does their very person play a central role? Early Buddhism insisted on the importance of the Buddha's teaching alone; moreover the developed doctrine of sunyata or emptiness went further and said that finally even the Buddha's teaching must be abandoned. As the second-century Buddhist, Nagarjuna stated: 'True bliss consists in the elimination and calming of all activity. Nowhere did Buddha teach anything whatsoever.'[16] As for the person of the Buddha, one guru is reported to have said, 'If you meet the Buddha, slay him,' meaning that one seeking perfection should not fasten on the person of the Buddha but go beyond him to nirvana and emptiness. Yet Mahayana Buddhism, as I have said, developed a religion and in this religion the Buddha was elevated to divine status, made an ontological absolute, and came to be viewed as a saviour-figure actively intervening in the lives of the faithful. In Jewish mystical tradition Moses, Abraham Abulafia, and Isaac Luria, to mention a few, are important teachers and examples, but the Jewish mystic is more interested in their teaching and example than in their persons. The same is true of Mohammed for the Sufis. Hindu tradition has its renowned mystic-teachers like Ramanuja, who are looked to only for their teaching and example, but it also has a doctrine of avatars or descents of the divinity, in which the divinity appears among men in accessible form for the good of mankind: the nineteenth-century Hindu, Ramakrishna, is considered such an avatar.[17] Christian mysticism for its part sees in Jesus Christ not only a great teacher and example but also a continually living and present *mediator* of the gifts that prepare and effect mystical experience and union. (There is, I might add, variation among some Christian mystics as to the place to be given in actual prayer to imagination of the humanity of Jesus.)

Still another question pointing up varieties of attitudes among and within mystical traditions is this: what is the relation of the mystic to society, to human effort and human history? Is it a withdrawal, a search to escape time and history in order to find peace and rest in the eternal, a quest for solitude, a denial of the validity or reality of society and of the value of its struggles and history? This attitude has been said to be found, for example, in Hinayana Buddhism and among some 'fundamentalist' kabbalists. Or is it an attitude of withdrawal in order to be a beacon and source of spiritual energy for society? This has been the attitude in both East and West of many monastic orders of contemplatives. Or does the mystic regard this gift as preparatory for his re-entry into society and its struggles in order

11

to help renew its spiritual energies and redirect its movement?
This last attitude is found among a number of mystics of the
western Christian tradition; it is prominent in Mahayana Buddhism
where it is best exemplified by its bodhisattvas, enlightened
persons who remain this side of nirvana, or of becoming Buddhas,
in order to help the suffering world to gain freedom from
affliction; Sufi mystics in the Muslim tradition have had a rich
tradition of service to their brethren, and many of the great
Hindu mystics have been outstanding servants of people and of
society.

I have no time to do more than mention several other important
questions related to mysticism that receive various answers. If
one accepts the validity of mystical experience, do criteria
exist for judging the genuine from the spurious, and if so, what
are they? (The simplest and best, I might venture, still seems
to be: 'By their fruits you shall know them'.) Again, what
relation is to be seen among the different mystical traditions:
assertion of fundamental differences and competition? an ignoring
of differences in uncritical syncretism an attempt at concord
amid difference? Mystics tend toward universalism and unity of
spirit, and yet there can and have been sharp differences both
practically and doctrinally.

Finally, what is the relation between outstanding periods of
mystical experience and the social and cultural context of such
periods? Here social historians, sociologist, and scholars of
historical mentalities can contribute greatly, and may have much
to tell us about the current renewed interest in mysticism that
this seminar exemplifies. What careful social analysis may show
(but this is only a guess at this stage) is that when a culture
or a society, and especially its religious bodies, diminish in
vitality and purpose and hope, there arises or the society is
given a thirst for, this more direct experiential knowledge and
love of God or Ultimate Reality. At such times sources of spiritual energy may well flow more abundantly to revitalize individuals and through them their society and culture.

We meet in a province whose rich dark soil gives rise to many
kinds of physical energy. But perhaps our seminar here in
Alberta can point beyond oil and gas and grain and cattle to
rich sources of spiritual energy that are far more important for
the survival and development of humanity. Indeed, one may ask
if the mystics are not the first among us to make a leap forward
that will one day draw all men and women to a higher state of
personal and social evolution. The words of Pierre Teilhard de
Chardin quoted in the *Encyclopaedia Brittanica* article on
mysticism may serve to remind us how important our subject and
seminar discussions are, and may point out the hopeful direction
in which mystics might be leading all of us:

The outcome of the world, the gates of the future, the entry
into the super-human -- these are not thrown open to a few of

12

the privileged nor to one chosen people to the exclusion of all others. They will open only to an advance of *all together* in a direction in which *all together* can find[18] and join completion in a spiritual renovation of the earth.

FOOTNOTES

1 *The New Yorker* 36/10 (23 April 1960) 43; republished in his *Everyone but Thee and Me* (Boston-Toronto: Little, Brown, 1962), p 146

2 *Webster's Third New International Dictionary of the English Language: Unabridged* (Springfield, Mass.: Merriam,1961) p 1497

3 See the back cover of Frits Staal *Exploring Mysticism* (Harmondsworth, England: Penguin: 1975) "Can mysticism be the subject of rational inquiry? It is commonly claimed — particularly in the West where science is deeply suspicious of mystical experience — that visions, occult powers and states of mind beyond the reach of reason cannot profitably be examined through the agency of reason." This of course is not a link or association made in the book by the author himself.

4 Paul Hellyer *The Sunday Sun* (Toronto) 11 July 1976 p 11

5 1 May 1976 p B8

6 Much of what follows on the meanings of "mystical" is based on Louis Bouyer "Mysticism An Essay on the History of a Word" in *Mystery and Mysticism: A Symposium*, ed. A. Plé (New York: Philosophical Library 1956) pp 119-137. See also A Plé "Mysticism and Mystery" ibid., pp 1-17 and G.W.H. Lampe, ed. *A Patristic Greek Lexicon* (Oxford: Clarendon, 1961-68) s.vv. μυστήριον and μυστικός, pp 891-94

7 One will recognize here the basic elements outlined by William James *The Varieties of Religious Experience* (1902 rpt. New York: Collier,1974) pp 299-301. J. Schoneberg Setzer "Making the Mystics Make Sense" *Spiritual Frontiers* 5 (1973) 226-45; 6 (1974) 21-40,80-88 draws on many studies to compile a list of fifteen characteristics of mystical experience (pp 228-30) that is interesting and helpful but in my opinion too particularized to include the experience as described in some traditions or by individuals within some traditions.

8 See Gershom G. Scholem *Major Trends in Jewish Mysticism*, 3rd ed. rev. (New York: Schocken, 1954; rpt. 1961) p 137, concerning Abulafia; and Teresa of Avila *Life*, ch. 20 in *The Complete Works of St. Teresa of Jesus*, 3 vols., trans. and ed. E. Allison Peers (London:Sheed and Ward,1972 rpt.1973) I,119-125; see also her *Spiritual Relations*, 5, ibid., I,327-31.

9 See Scholem, p 17

10 "Some Psychological Foundations of Meditation Techniques,
    Newsletter-Review 8/1-2 (Spring 1976) p 4. (This review is
    published by the R.M. Bucke Memorial Society for the Study of
    Religious Experience, 4453 Maisonneuve Blvd., West, Montreal.)

11 Quoted in Annemarie Schimmel *Mystical Dimensions of Islam*
    (Chapel Hill: University of North Carolina Press,1975) p 2

12 For the first pair see H.C. Gardiner and E.E. Larkin "Mysticism
    in Literature" *New Catholic Encyclopedia* 10 (1968) 179; for the
    second pair see Schimmel, p 5

13 In conversation with me during the conference, however, Swami
    Prabuddhananda modified this frequently expressed view of
    Shankara. Students of Shankara he told me form this opinion
    because they concentrate on his commentaries on the scriptures
    but neglect his hymns and prayers which reveal love and
    devotion in his mysticism.

14 *Fragments of the Future Scroll* (Germantown: Leaves of Grass,
    1975) p 29

15 *Major Trends*, p 6

16 Quoted in Thomas Berry *Religions of India: Hinduism, Yoga,
    Buddhism* (New York:Burce; London:Collier-Macmillan 1971) p 173

17 On Ramanuja (12th century) see A.M. Esnoul *Ramanuja et la mys-
    tique vishnouite* 'Maîtres Spirituels' 32 (Paris:Seuil 1964);on
    Ramakrishna see Solange Lemaître *Râmakrishna et la vitalité de
    l'hindouisme* "Maîtres spirituels" 18 (Paris:Seuil 1975)

18 See Sisir Kumar Ghose "Mysticism" *Encyclopaedia Brittanica*, 15
    ed., *Macropaedia* 12,793:he gives the first part (ending at the
    first 'all together'). The full text is from *The Phenomenon
    of Man* (London:Collins,1959) pp 244-45 where in a note Teil-
    hard remarks about his phrase 'all together': "Even if they do
    so only under the influence of a few, an élite."

THE NATURE OF MYSTICISM

AS PERSONALLY EXPERIENCED

My Spiritual Discipline
By BROTHER DAVID STEINDL-RAST

The key word of the Spiritual discipline I follow is "listening".
This means a special kind of listening, a listening with one's
heart. To listen in that way is central to the monastic tradition in which I stand. The very first word of the Rule of St.
Benedict is "listen!" -- "Ausculta!" -- and all the rest of
Benedictine discipline grows out of this one initial gesture of
wholehearted listening, as a sunflower grows from its seed.

Benedictine spirituality in turn is rooted in the broader and
more ancient tradition of the Bible. But here, too, the concept
of listening is central. In the biblical vision all things are
brought into existence by God's creative Word; all of history
is a dialogue with God who speaks to the human heart. The Bible
has been admired for proclaiming with great clarity that God is
One and Transcendent. Yet, the still more admirable insight of
the religious genius reflected in biblical literature is the
insight that God speaks. The transcendent God communicates Self
through nature and through history. The human heart is called
to listen and to respond.

Responsive listening is the form which the Bible gives to our
basic religious quest as human beings. This is the quest for a
full human life, for happiness. It is the quest for meaning,
for our happiness hinges not on good luck; it hinges on peace
of heart. Even in the midst of what we call bad luck, in the
midst of pain and suffering, we can find peace of heart, if we
find meaning in it all. Biblical tradition points the way by
proclaiming that God speaks to us in and through even the most
troublesome predicaments. By listening deeply to the message
of any given moment I shall be able to tap the very Source of
Meaning and to realize the unfolding meaning of my life.

To listen in this way means to listen with one's heart, with
one's whole being. The heart stands for that center of our
being at which we are truly "together". Together with ourselves,
not split up into intellect, will, emotions, into mind and body.
Together with all other creatures, for the heart is that realm
where I am paradoxically not only most intimately myself, but
most intimately united with all. Together with God, the source
of life, the life of my life, welling up in the heart. In order
to listen with my heart, I must return again and again to my heart
through a process of centering, through taking things to heart.
Listening with my heart I will find meaning. For just as the
eye perceives light and the ear sound, the heart is the organ
for meaning.

MY SPIRITUAL DISCIPLINE

The daily discipline of listening and responding to meaning is
called obedience. This concept of obedience is far more compre-
hensive than the narrow notion of obedience as doing-what-you-
are-told-to-do. Obedience in the full sense is the process of
attuning the heart to the simple call contained in the complexity
of a given situation. The only alternative is absurdity. "Ab-
surdus" literally means absolutely deaf. If I call a situation
absurd I admit that I am deaf to its meaning. I admit implicitly
that I must become "ob-audiens" - thoroughly listening, obedient.
I must give my ear, give myself, so fully to the word that reaches
me that it will send me. Being sent by the word, I will be obedient to my mission. Thus, by doing the truth lovingly, not by
analyzing it, will I begin to understand.

The ethical implications of all this are obvious. Therefore it
is all the more important to remember that we are not primarily
concerned with an ethical but with a religious matter; not primarily with purpose, even the most exalted purpose of good works,
but with that religious dimension from which every purpose must
derive its meaning. The Bible calls the responsive listening
of obedience "living by the Word of God", and that means far more
than merely doing God's will. It means being nourished by God's
word as food and drink, God's word in every person, every thing,
every event.

This is a daily task, a moment by moment discipline. I eat a
tangerine and the resistance of the rind, as I peel it, speaks
to me, if I am alert enough. Its texture, its fragrance speaks
an intranslatable language, which I have to learn. Beyond the
awareness that each little segment has its own degree of sweet-
ness (the ones on the side that was exposed to the sun are the
sweetest) lies the awareness that all this is pure gift. Or
could one ever deserve such food?

I hold a friend's hand in mine, and this gesture becomes a word
the meaning of which goes far beyond words. It makes demands
on me. It is an implicit pledge. It calls for faithfulness and
for sacrifice. But it is above all a celebration of friendship,
a meaningful gesture that need not be justified by any practical
purpose. It is as superfluous as a sonnet or a string quartet,
as superfluous as all the ultimately important things in life.
It is a word of God by which I live.

But a calamity is also word of God when it hits me. While working for me, a young man, as dear to me as my own little brother,
has an accident. Glass is shattered in his eyes and I find him
lying blindfolded in a hospital bed. What is God saying now?
Together we grope, grapple, listen, strain to hear. Is this, too,
a lifegiving word? When we can no longer make sense of a given
situation, we have reached the crucial point. Now arises the
challenge that calls for faith.

20

The clue lies in the fact that any given moment confronts us with a given reality. But if it is given, it is gift. If it is gift, the appropriate response is thanksgiving. Yet, thanksgiving, where it is genuine, does not primarily look at the gift and express appreciation; it looks at the giver and expresses trust. The courageous confidence which trusts in the Giver of all gifts is faith. To give thanks even when we cannot see the goodness of the gift, trusting in the goodness of the Giver, - to learn this is to find the path to peace of heart. For happiness is not what makes us grateful. It is gratefulness that makes us happy.

In a lifelong process the discipline of listening teaches us to live "by *every* word that proceeds from the mouth of God" without discrimination. We learn this by "giving thanks in *all* things." The monastery is an environment set up to facilitate just that. The method is detachment. When we fail to distinguish between wants and needs we lose sight of our goal. Our needs (many of them imaginary) keep increasing; our gratefulness (and so our happiness) dwindles. Monastic discipline reverses this course. The monk strives for needing less and less while becoming more and more grateful.

Detachment decreases our needs. The less we have, the easier it is gratefully to appreciate what we do have. Silence creates the atmosphere for detachment. Silence pervades monastic life in the same way in which noise pervades life elsewhere. Silence creates space around things, persons and events. Silence singles them out and allows us gratefully to consider them one by one in their uniqueness. Leisure is the discipline of finding time to do so. Leisure is the expression of detachment with regard to time. For the leisure of monks is not the privilege of those who can afford to take time; it is the virtue of those who give to everything they do the time it deserves to take.

Within the monastery the listening which is the essence of this spiritual discipline expresses itself in bringing life into harmony with the cosmic rhythm of seasons and hours, with "time, not our time" as T.S. Eliot calls it. But in my personal life, obedience often demands that I serve outside the monastery. What counts is the listening to the soundless bell of "time, not our time", wherever it be and the doing of whatever needs to be done when it is time--" now, and in the hour of our death". "And the time of death is every moment", says T.S. Eliot, because the moment in which we truly listen is "a moment in and out of time."

One method for entering moment by moment into that mystery is the discipline of the Jesus Prayer, the Prayer of the Heart, as it is also called. It consists basically in the mantric repetition of the name of Jesus, synchronized with one's breath and heartbeat. When I repeat the name of Jesus at a given moment in time, I make that moment transparent to the Now that does not pass away. The whole biblical notion of living by the Word is summed up in the name of Jesus in whom I as a Christian a- dore the Word incarnate. By giving that name to every thing and to every person I encounter, by invoking it in every situation in which I find myself, I remind myself that everything is just another way of spelling out the inexhaustible fulness of the one eternal word of God, the Logos; I remind my heart to listen.

This image might seem to suggest a dualistic rift between God who speaks and the obedient heart. Yet, the dualistic tension is caught up and transcended in the mystery of the Trinity. In the light of that mystery I understand myself as a word spoken out of the Creator's heart and at the same time addressed by the Creator. But the communion goes deeper. In order to understand the word addressed to me, the word I am, I must speak the lan- guage of the One who calls. If I can understand God at all this can come about only by my sharing in God's own Spirit of Self- understanding. Thus the responsive listening in which my spiritual discipline consists is not dualistic communication. It is the celebration of triune communion: the Word, coming forth from Silence, leads by Understanding home into Silence. My heart, like a vessel thrown into the ocean, is filled with God's life and totally immersed in it. All this is pure gift. It remains for me to rise to the occasion by all-embracing thanksgiving.

Spiritual Disciplines of a Practising Mystic
According to Hinduism
By SWAMI PRABUDDHANANDA

"Religion is the eternal relationship between the eternal soul
and the eternal God." The soul and God are both by nature pure,
enlightened, free and blissful. There is an inseparable, eternal
connection between them. That means everyone is a potential
mystic. One whom we generally call a mystic has realized this
fact in his own life, or has had glimpses which go beyond
intellectual conviction or emotional satisfaction.

Systematic and continuous practice is necessary to have this
experience. The results of this practice are described in different ways, as removal of ignorance regarding one's real nature,
and that of the world, as complete effacement of the ego, or as
desirelessness. Positively, spiritual practice brings awareness of the Spirit within and without, and awakens love for God
and man. In the process character is formed, mind controlled
and the spirit of service increased. One attains peace, and
becomes fearless.

Moral discipline is the foundation of spiritual practices.
Virtues like truthfulness, chastity, self-control, duty-con-
sciousness, etc. are not only necessary but should be culti-
vated throughout spiritual life. The life of a practising mystic
has two aspects – negative and positive. He negates the wrong
ways of thinking, feeling, and acting and asserts the closeness
or identity with Reality at every step. His ideal is realization of the Self or God and welfare of the world considering
it as the embodiment of God. His whole life is centered around
this. He regulates his life accordingly.

Study of and reflection on the scriptures is an important
factor in a spiritual seeker's life. He must expose himself as
much as possible to the ideas and teachings of great teachers and
illumined souls. Their words are infused with spiritual power,
and they should be deeply impressed upon the heart and mind of
a seeker. The inner personality has to be soaked with spiritual
thoughts and feelings in order that a transformation of character
can take place. Spiritural study is a great help in filling the
mind with such thoughts.

The aspirant gets inspiration and guidance from the great in-
carnations of God like Krishna, Buddha, Jesus etc. and also
from lesser teachers. The teacher is a friend and a companion
to the disciple. He also transmits spiritual power to the
student through the mantra. Through his loving guidance, com-
passion, and concern for the disciple, the teacher brings him
to the feet of God. The selfless love that fills the heart of
the teacher aids in forming an unbreakable bond and an intimate
relationship with the student.

He learns from the experiences of past men of knowledge that
Reality is one and one alone, and the individual soul and God

are the same in essence. Based on their experiences and his own reasoning, the practising mystic discriminates continuously between the real (that which is eternal) and the unreal (that which is non-eternal). He clings to the Reality and cultivates dispassion or non-attachment for the passing or temporary things of life.

"Truth is one; sages call it by various names." The forms of God are numerous. A spiritual seeker is asked, in the beginning, to choose an aspect or a form of God with the help of a teacher. This becomes his Chosen Ideal. The teacher gives a Divine name (mantra), and instructions for meditation. The scattered mind is withdrawn from outside objects and is turned inward. The disciple repeats the Divine name and meditates on its meaning in his heart. Meditation is a constant flow of loving thought towards the Self-effulgent Spirit. He thus tries to contact the Supreme Spirit in an intimate way. Prayer is offered to the Lord for right understanding, illumination, purity and other spiritual qualities. Prayer is also offered for the welfare of fellow beings. Chanting, and singing of songs and hymns are also done, according to the temperament of an individual.

As the aspirant grows, his conception of God expands, and he no longer simply visualizes the form and feels the Divine Presence within, but also gradually begins to see Him in everything. He moves from a small idea of God to a larger and yet larger one until he merges in the Infinite. A devotee through a relationship with God is brought into close contact with Him. All fear and awe vanish. The heart is purified, and is filled with love for the Beloved.

A spiritual seeker may adopt different attitudes towards the world. He may view it as his own Self. He may consider himself and everyone as sparks of the Divine. He may feel that he is a child of the Divine Father or Mother and likewise all others. Thus, he is connected with everyone through the Divine, just as bubbles and waves are connected to one another through the ocean. He tries to contact the world in and through the Spirit. Love for man is grounded in love for God. Because man's real nature is Divine, it is the Divine responding to the Divine. "Verily, not for the sake of the husband is the husband dear but a husband is dear for the sake of the Self. Verily, not for the sake of the wife is the wife dear but a wife is dear for the sake of the Self. Verily, not for the sake of the sons are the sons dear but the sons are dear for the sake of the Self. Verily, not for the sake of the beings are the beings dear but the beings are dear for the sake of the Self."

Service to humanity is done as a spiritual practice, as worship. It may be physical, intellectual, moral or spiritual, or all these according to the capacity and temperament of the aspirant and the need of the recipient. Any action has the

24

potential of revealing Divinity. Every being in the relative world is compelled by nature internal and external to act. He therefore performs action, experiences the result and becomes subject to bondage through desire and attachment. So, in order to spiritualize action, certain techniques have to be employed. The science of work or karma yoga is elaborately dealt with in the Bhagavad Gita. Sri Krishna, spiritual teacher par excellence, points out to his disciple Arjuna: "The world becomes bound by action unless it be done with the spirit of dedication. Therefore, O son of Kunti, give up attachment and do your work for the sake of the Lord." Here Krishna is not suggesting renunciation of action, but renunciation in action. He says that one should work as an instrument in the hands of God with non-attachment, renouncing the fruits of action, but then adds one should dedicate all actions as well as oneself to the Divine. "Surrendering in thought all actions to Me, regarding Me as the Supreme Goal and practising steadiness of mind, fix your heart O Arjuna, constantly on Me." Another way of achieving non-attachment is by working as a witness. One performs action knowing it is the Divine Power that is performing all action while the Self of man remains unaffected. When there is no desire, or hankering after results, action is then performed for its own sake or for others, and not for any ulterior motive. This type of work is possible only when there is sameness, or evenness of mind. Through the practice of equanimity of mind, one is filled with peace. "Therefore always do without attachment the work you have to do; for a man who does his work without attachment attains the Supreme."

All these spiritual disciplines are practised by the same individual according to the need and mood, but those of different temperaments may emphasize certain practices. The ideal is to give equal importance to all the disciplines so that one may supplement and balance the others. In this way the personality is integrated and perfection is reached.

Fasting, observing silence, occasionally seeking solitude, pilgrimage, formal external worship, celebrations of the birthdays of saints and spiritual teachers are undertaken according to particular needs and convenience. Taking vows also helps one commit oneself fully and steadfastly to the ideal.

As one progresses in spiritual life, one feels the guiding and helping hand of God. The Lord showers His grace on the seeker and he makes rapid strides towards the Divine. "The Breeze of Divine grace is always blowing, but you have to unfurl your sails."

Zen Mystical Practice
By EIDO ROSHI

Good morning. When I was asked to participate in this conference, the first thing that I asked myself was whether or not
I was a mystic. The answer, the honest answer, was that it
seems that I am not. I shall explain later why I am not. If I
should shave my head as I have done, wear a black robe as I have
now, and perhaps if I kept silent and not talked, I may impress
you as if I were different from you, and thereby, you may consider me a mystic. But, here, I am sitting in front of you and
am obliged to say something about mysticism; at that moment,
my category of mystic is lost. That is one aspect. But at the
same time, as Brother David and Swami Prabuddhananda have mentioned, to the extent that we are alive and are not satisfied with
just the material things in life and through our capacities seek
for something or try something, to that extent there is no
human being who is not a mystic. So we are mystics, "Yes!"
and we are mystics, "No!"

In any case, I was asked to say something about the nature of
mysticism as personally experienced by me, which in my case is
Zen Buddhism.

In general, there are five steps involved in the practice of
Zen Buddhism which I follow. The five steps are:

1. understanding,
2. belief,
3. practice,
4. realization, and
5. integration.

Now, the first. Understanding takes place in our daily conversation, in hearing lectures, in reading books, and in finding
out that there is something of experience which, in the human
language, may be called "mysticism." The more we read, the more
we hear, and the more we search, we come to the conclusion that
"Yes, there is, there may be such a thing!" but this understanding, the first step of Zen Buddhism, is not mysticism itself. Do you follow me? If such were the case, university studies, from anthropology to mathematics and physics, would have be
be mysticism, and that would result in too much mysticism.

Now, how about the second step, belief? Perhaps, it would
be better to say "conviction" than "belief." When intellectual
understanding is well accepted and becomes more than intellectual
understanding, then we want to believe. It is this belief that
leads us to the next step. Although without conviction, we are
too lazy to try to advance, this "conviction" or "belief" cannot,

I think, be considered "mysticism".   So the first two
steps of Zen Buddhism are not mystical at all.

How about the third, practise? In the English language, we
say, for example, "Practise the piano." I do not think that
practising the piano is a mystical experience. We say, "Practise
law as a lawyer." Well, I don't think that is mysticism either.
We say, "Practise meditation." Then all of a sudden, this is
slightly different. We start to wonder and perhaps think that
this is something mysterious. Some of us may think that the
practise of meditation belongs to the category of mysticism.
But is it really so or not? When one sits down on a chair or
on a cushion, with an erect spine and regulated breath, this is
very realistic and not at all mystical. So practise, practise
of meditation, is still not within the category of mysticism.
Three out of five - the majority - do not belong to mysticism.

The fourth, realization. Now it is this category that I cannot
reject as being a mystical experience. It is mystical from an
ordinary point of view, but from the mystical point of view, it is
not at all mysterious. Do you understand? From the ordinary
point of view, it sounds so mysterious, but from an experience
itself point of view, what we generally call "the ordinary point
of view" is more mysterious than the mystical experience itself.
This is true. That experience has been described by many distinguished scholars and mystics in various ways, so there is no
need for me to repeat it, but the significance of testifying to
such an unique state of mind makes our lives much richer. But
that is not all.

The fifth step is called integration. We eat food, digest it,
and make it our energy. But we have to eat again, because we
become hungry. In the same manner, we have to repeat this
series of practise, realization, and integration again and again.
There is no end in this mystic path. People think that enlightenment is an experience, but enlightenment is not an experience. It is an insight. Through this insight and through
the infusion or integration, one can express oneself in different ways - aesthetically, poetically, realistically, or some other
way. This is the point at which the so-called "mystical practise"
and the so-called "human society" or "human life" meet. Because
people do not understand this "integration," mystics are often
misunderstood. People say that they are not productive or that
they are just escaping. Indeed they are not productive in the
ordinary sense, but they are productive in that they produce
the great integration.

Now I shall add a few things. How does this practice take
place? In Zen Buddhist tradition, the main thing is to sit --
especially, on the floor, in a state in which one is united with
his breath. In the Japanese or Chinese languages, this breath
is called "*iki*". The character for *iki* consists of two parts:

28

one part is called "self" and the lower part is called "mind."
Breath is therefore, "self-mind." So when we sit, we regulate
our minds. What we do is simply called "concentration." But
concentration really means purification, and purification means
to remove unnecessary defilements. For example, when we want
to clean up this room, we do not bring anything in, but rather,
we remove this table, this microphone, this chair and so on until everything is removed. When this is done, then we bring in
a vacuum cleaner and remove the tiny particles of dust. When this
is done, this room is very, very clean -- purified . In the same
way, our minds, from the time we are born, have collected a lot
of junk. Because of this junk, we have problems. The practice
of meditation is a junk removing process. However, when we
state it in a more beautiful term, we call it "purification."

In order to purify our minds, we use nothing more than our
own breath. We sit with erect posture so that we can unite
better with Heaven and with earth. In this way, we go into a
special state of mind, which unfortunately is indescribable.

What more can I say? I shall conclude my talk.

The Humanistic Transcendentalist Practice of the Kabbalah
By RABBI ZALMAN SCHACHTER

The humanistic transcendentalist wants to achieve the highest
level of religious intensity without feeling compelled to develop
fanaticism at the same time. True, all the evidence of the past
points to their inseparability.   Yet the working hypothesis
of our humanist is that not only is religious depth without
fanaticism desirable, but that it *must* be achieved. He, therefore, seeks, among other things, to enter into a dialogue of
devoutness with seekers of other faiths, comparing ways,
techniques and methods of how to focus awareness on God, how
to make prayer life more relevant and effective, and how to
become a clearer and better channel for the light.

He is a humanist because the enterprise of human beings
contacting the Cosmic Mind is of great concern to him. He
realizes that all revelation is as much a function of the re-
vealer as it is the function of the seeker. The Divine Re-
vealer depends on man for the keyboard on which to play His
revelation. The content of the symphony, the revelation, is
limited by the range of the instruments: the consciousness
of the seeker's mind. The phenomena which psychology discusses
under the category of set and setting determine the focus, the
scale of observation, the depth of field, as well as the
sensitivity of the human instrument.

This humanism is not new to Torah. The sages referred to
it in terms of the Torah speaking in the language of man.
The Humanist knows, however, that even the conditions of his
set, setting, sensitivity, and so on are the results of the
unfolding of the Divine plan. He does not cut himself off
from the Divine Immanence which produced him in the here-and-
now. As he participates in the process of revelation (a
mutuality akin to love-making) his contribution to the process
is no less important and ecstasy-producing than that of his
Divine partner. (For this reason kabbalists even of the
fundamentalist variety speak of this dialogue as the con-
junction between the Holy One, blessed be He, and His female
Sh'khinah.) Still he makes an act of faith and unification,
recognizing that on the monistic level even his own contribution is Divine. For this reason we think of him not only as
humanistic, but also as transcendalist.

He is a kabbalist because he respects the process in which
not only his mind, but those of all his predecessors, interact
with God. In studying their interactions with the Divine, he

is no less turned on than the lover who sets his own inner stage
by reading erotic literature. Looking at Simon Bar Yochai of
the *Zohar*, Abraham Abulafia, Cordovero, Luria of Safed, and the
hassidic masters, our humanistic kabbalist is prepared to receive
the Divine influx in himself. This, for him, is of supreme
value. He immerses himself in the literature to the extent of
his ability, in the original if he is capable, or in what is
available in translation if not. And because he is a humanist,
he immerses himself not only in Jewish sources, but also in
those coming from other traditions which arouse him to greater
receptivity of the cosmic.
    Humanistic psychology, as well as its closely allied neighbor,
transpersonal psychology, are for him arsenals of psychic tools.
Gestalt, from its first academic figure-ground application to
its therapeutic intra-personal flips, allow him to change places
with God in his inner life.

    Carnality is no threat to the humanist. Having resensitized
himself, often at great personal cost in therapy, he has
managed to set aside some of the sabotage which society and the
school system have inflicted upon him. When he tastes food,
or becomes aware of a fragrance, or enjoys the harmonies of
sight and sound, or the tender feeling generated by touch, he
may actually be saying "Thank God!" more than the hundred times
per day that the Law requires blessings to be recited. He is
moved to profound meditation on the *S'firot* when giving or
receiving a massage. Massaging the right arm and right section
of the chest and back, he can contact, in his consciousness,
the Divine attribute of *Ḥesed* and thus can follow the Tree of
the *S'firot* over the entire body. When we ask him how he
construes this "holy carnality," he might respond by explicating
Scripture:
    "Um'vasair ehzeh Elohah","From my flesh I see God."
The verb used here is not *er'eh*, "I shall see clearly or
objectively", but *ehzeh*, a verb used to denote inner
vision, prophecy. The Divine name *Elohah* is not the name
of any particular attribute, but the undifferentiated God
available to vision through my body. From my right hand
I can envision *YHVH* (the indescribably Beautiful One,
T'feret), and so forth, through the various parts of the
body.
    When my body is in the right tone, alive, aware and
tingling, such vision becomes possible. I am in touch
with my vehicle and I can visualize the Divine, being in
touch with His Name. When I am aware of my breath -
breathing in - I am in touch with *N'shamah* (my soul) and
the world of *B'riyah* (the Spirit) and the world of *Yezirah,*
and when I breath out I'm in touch with *Nefesh* (animation)

and the world of *Assiah*, (function).

To put it differently: When I am in my head, I am in the letter *Yud* of the Divine Name *YHVH* and in the world of *Azilut*. When I am in my chest and arms and am aware of my breath, I am in the letter *He*, a breath letter, and in *B'riyah*. When I'm in my spine going from the base to the top, I am in the letter *Vav* and the world of *Y'zirah*, and when I am in my legs and pelvis I am in the letter *He*, the final one in the Name and in the world of *Assiyah*.

In becoming aware of these significances, I begin to realize that the body is not only the Temple of the spirit but it is my special altar to God to serve Him when tasting and feeling. I can, thereby, give back to Him the gift of my particular sensations.

The humanist's carnality is integrated with his spirituality.

What then is our bias? We want all the benefits to our interior life which we can gain from as close an identification as we can manage with the fundamentalist kabbalist. We will, for the sake of entering into the tryst of consciousness with God, suspend our critical dis-belief. Somewhere in the back of our minds we will also hold on to the rich storehouse of information concerning historical data and context of the Kabbalah which we received from the behaviouristic historian of Kabbalah. But most of all, we are committed to be in the here-and-now with an eye to move the center to the periphery, and the periphery to the center, thus turning the here into everywhere, and the now into the eternal present.

What are our tools? In communicating with one another we often face the problem of not meeting in the same universe of discourse. The nomenclature of the Kabbalah provides us with a *roadmap of consciousness*.

A KABBALAH ROADMAP OF CONSCIOUSNESS

(DIVINE ATTRIBUTE) s'firot	world	part of the service	soul aspect	letter of divine name	
HOKHMAH	AZILUTH	AMIDAH	HAYAH	YOD	ASCENT AND RETURN THROUGH DAILY PRAYER
---	--- ego barrier ---	---	---	---	
BINAH	B'RIYAH	SHMA and blessings	NESHAMAH	HEH	
S'FIROT	YEZIRAH	PSUQEY D"ZIMRA	RU'AH	VAV	
MALKHUT	ASSIYAH (spiritual)	QORBANOT	NEFESH	HEH	
	ASSIYAH	BLESSINGS OVER BODY FUNCTIONS BIRKHOT HASHAHAR	PHYSICAL BODY	ADNY	

What do we mean by worlds? We will be talking of higher
worlds and lower worlds. "High" and "low" are conveniences,
habits of language acquired over a long time. We only borrow
these terms and they will continue to sound as if special
dimensions are meant, but it is not necessary to remind the
reader that where inner spaces are concerned "low" and "high"
intermingle on our plane of reality like low and high fre-
quencies of the radio band. God-realization, however, is
possible in any one of those worlds, high or low.

The world of physical reality is known as *"Physical Assiah"*.
In it, we do the kind of work for which we have to be paid.
We have no emotional investment in it one way or another. The
seeker resides in this world with skillful equanimity. Looking
at the line for "Physical *Assiah*" on the "Worlds" Chart we see
that it represents function in the world of action. The
electro-magnetic spectrum of matter, waves and particles
represent the action and the actors. The physical body is
grounded in it. The element of *earth* and the *mineral kingdom*
are ways of reflecting the substance of this world. It is the
consciousness of the complete *rasha* of the *Tanya*. The Torah
consciousness it engenders is mostly mechanical and deals with
grammar and vocabulary.

As we proceed upward on the chart, we now enter three
spiritual universes, one "higher" than the other; the worlds
of spiritual *Assiah, Y'zirah* and *B'riyah*. We now can follow
the chart according to the different columns, each one in-
dicating the hierarchy of that particular dimension. Following, for example, the aspects of the soul, where the physical
body was located in physical *Assiah* , we find *Nefesh* on the
level of spiritual *Assiah*. In the Kabbalah, "soul" has several
names, each one corresponding to a different aspect of soul.
In *Y'zirah*, we find *Ru'ah*, and on the level of *B'riyah,* we find
N'shamah. In the spiritual realm we can go no higher than
B'riyah. Transcending, however, the ego barrier, which no
created object can pass, by opening the door of transcendence,
we may be able to find ourselves taken up to the soul level of
Hayah in the world of *Azilut*.

Experientially, the world of spiritual *Assiah* is one where we
do the kind of function that is so skilled that we need no other
reward. Of this, the sages spoke when they said "the reward of
the *mizvah* is the *mizvah* itself." On that level, the only
intention that matters is that the devotee see his function as
doing God's will. The *S'firot* of *Malkhut* calls on him to accept
the yoke of the Kingdom of Heaven. However, usually other
motivations accompany the doing of a *mizvah*. On the level of
Yezirah and *Ru'ah*, he also feels the influence of the *S'firot*
charging him with emotional energies of love and awe. The consciousness of the world of *Y'zirah* is that of the fervent

devotee. However, even this motivation for doing a *miẓvah* is
further charged by an intellectual motivation that derives
from the world of *B'riyah*. The soul aspect of *N'shamah* is not
satisfied by the emotions alone. Yearning for cosmic perspective, nothing less than the ability to perceive patterns
connecting alpha to omega, with everything in between, satisfies
him who worships God with his mind. He is the one who meditates
at great length on the meaning of everything. He deals in
signification and communicates with others in terms of integrated
signification. In doing a *miẓvah*, *N'shamah* rides on the general
obedience to God of *Nefesh*, on the emotional fervor of *Ru'ah*,
and charges the act with significance of thought. The *N'shamah*
lives in the world of *B'riyah*. *B'riyah* is energized by the
S'firot of *B'riyah*, which seeks to understand everything in
detail and specificity. This understanding is very far from
the ego-heavy conceptualisation.   On the contrary, it participates with the *seraphim*, angelic mind entities, in an ego-
less contemplation of God-in-the-universe-and-history. While
the *N'shamah* finds fulfillment in this intellection, it yearns
even further to transcend this sublime mentation and courts its
own annihilation, seeking to transcend itself by manifesting
its divine core, *Hayah*. A *miẓvah* done with *Hayah* manifesting
is no longer doing someone else's will, but rather it is the
divine will doing itself through the vehicle of the now ego-
less devotee.

In the kabbalistic version of the ascent the worlds of *Assiyah*
yezirah and *Briyah* are basically creature worlds and as such
where they are real the divine is hidden. Not so in the world
of *Azilut (Brahma Loka?)* there creature cannot reach and only
G-d is and S/He/It is only subject being *I am* and not object
being (object existing as an entity). Persons - souls are not
created but begotten and of the same substance -- if this word
can be borrowed - as the Divine being. The soul is not aware of
there being more than one Being in *Azilut*; there is only One and
no other and the soul is a moment of G-d. All awareness of this
moment is only a dim reflection of that nonbeing-being which is
real in *Azilut* and leaves only an after amnesia reflection in
the world of *B'riyah*.

Each one of these Universes of discourse has its own way of
being real and the laws applying in one world do not of necessity
apply in another.

Modern or scholastic philosophy of religion does not honor the
different levels of reality and their different laws. Yet the
experience of *Yezirah* is for me radically different than that of
B'riyah. *Yezirah* is dialogical, *Briyah* is conceptual, *Assyah* is
functional and works in the third person and with objects.
Azilut is unitive, all in the Divine subject, and admits one

only after what St. John of the Cross called the dark night of the soul.

SOME CONCLUDING PERSONAL COMMENTS

PRACTICE

My practice is not restricted to the times of prayer and meditation. All acts are performed in the presence of G-d as He is both within the soul and in the world. Special times for inner audit are also part of my practice. Liturgically the outer part of my practice follows along lines of orthodox Judaism.

EXPERIENCES

There is in me a hesitancy to put extra ordinary experiences "vouch safed" me at special grace moments into words. In order to present them to an audience not acquainted with the language of Kabbalah I would have to extract them from their context, pretty them up, make circular insight straight, reduce a cosmic insight to a good word, and try in some form to make them behave nicely in the presence of strangers. It would also require concepts that would become respectable G-d talk for professional philosophers - or better *sophologists*.

But this will not do. The *Sufis* have a word for it; *Madjdoob*-madman. One dervish seeing an other and recognizing in him an authentic moment will call out *Madjdoob*. Because in the depth of the experience there is what on this plane is madness. The law of the excluded middle is violated in the conjunctio oppositorum and paper is surely not the means of getting in touch with the other's point of madness (which alone can confirm the truth of core mystical states and statements).

TORAH

This pillar of the world (the others are Devotion to G-d and Service to humanity) makes study and conceptual work a holy act. The human mind becomes merged with the Divine. Most of the literature discussed by Scholem is that aspect of Torah in Kabbalah. In moments of light when pure essence flows through the soul the experience is not accessible to words and thus not available to verbal recall. Because of this amnesia sets in and I cannot reach that moment in my memory. Furthermore, it has an ear mark of its own authenticity and that is that it is always in the *PRESENT*, always right *NOW*. Only with difficulty can I train myself to recall that non-verbal flow to

process it in my awareness and digest in into my symbol structure,
prayer and moral life on this plane. I must do this detailed
home work or else I cannot enter the holy place again. The plane
on which this homework is done is the level and the consciousness
of Torah. But the observer must be aware and not confuse the
experience with the device for turning it into processable Torah
material. Here is where the language of the kabbalah is also a
hermenuetic of the manifestation of the ineffable. Kabbalah not
only allows for a way to recall these experiences but also
allows for their anticipation. Whenever Kabbalah study is *not*
accompanied by the primary experience of Divine reality it
atrophies into just another symbol system. When made potent by
experience it becomes apparent that the words used in kabbalah
are indeed pointing to a secret, a mystery and in this sense
while much of the kabbalah can be spoken about it tells nothing
but words to one who lacks the experience. Still initiation
into experience is a function of the preparation of the
psychological set engendered by the language. This way is open
to me via the Torah which, when the ground has been prepared by
understanding and study and meditation, enters into life in
order to Hallow it.

Lastly I wish to share one more point about *songs and hymns*.
There is a controversy between Buber and Scholem about the proper
way to present Hassidism. Buber's position is that the most
telling thing is to tell the tales of a masters life. One learns
most from the concrete situation. He often quoted R'Leib Sures
who said I come to my master to learn from him how he ties his
shoe laces. Scholem on the other hand argues that when a
teacher gave his teachings in talks and literary productions
these must be taken even more seriously than the tales. For
instance Buber's view on Levi Yitzhaq of Berditchev, which sees
him as an ecstatic, tends to ignore his opus magnum. The
Qedushat Levi shows Levi Yitzhaq to be a daring and clearly
reasoning teacher who writes in a noble rabbinic style -- rather
than, as Buber impresses us, someone only given to vernacular
outpourings. Lately it has become clear to me that both Buber and
Scholem ignore an essential dimension in the area of Jewish
Mysticism; that of the Tzaddik as a master of Prayer. For as
the elder Abraham Yehoshua Heshel of Apt (Prof. Heschel's great
grandfather) put it, prayer can only be learned from a praying
person.
If Stace could have read the hymns of the Kabbalists and (so
called) philosophers of the Middle Ages he would not have
questioned their validity as mystics. How much more so had he
been able to hear them sing and tune in to their consciousness.
In my own way I received the deepest transmissions from my Masters
the rabbis of Lubavitch and Bobov in prayer services which they

led.   There the spirit and Presence became manifest, validating
and verifying all that they had said in words and shown in
example.
Let me now sing for you.

SCHOLARLY ASSESSMENTS

OF

MYSTICISM

Mystical Experience as Cognition
By JOHN HICK

I.

Our 'practising mystics' have spoken both of mystical experience
and of the mystic's practices and disciplines. I should like to
discuss the former, the religious experience and its significance, rather than the practices and techniques which serve it.
Mystical experience, as our mystics (and others as well) describe
it, does not seem to me to be anything other than first-hand
religious experience as such. This is however, I believe, the
core of religion. Religion has often been understood, particularly within our modern science-oriented western culture, as an
attempt (though a primitive and unsuccessful attempt) to explain
certain puzzling phenomena, from perennial puzzles concerning
the origin of the world and the source of its order, to cosmic
puzzles concerning the origin of the world and the source of its
order, to local puzzles about why the rains are late this year
or what last night's thunder signified. There is, certainly,
an explanatory side to religion, although recent religious
thought has tended to apply these explanatory resources to the
existence or the meaning of the world as a whole rather than
to the occurrence of particular events within it. How far this
movement away from a theological explanation of the genesis of
particular events can or should be taken is an important open
question which, however, I shall not be taking up here. The
point I wish to make is rather that the explanatory function of
religion is secondary and derivative. Religion consists
primarily in experiencing our life in its relation to the
Transcendent and living on the basis of that experience. And
mysticism, I take it, is simply religion understood in this way.
Or, rather, it is a name for one, but the most important, aspect
of the total phenomenon of religion. In terms of Ninian Smart's
six-dimensional analysis - distinguishing the ritual, mytholo-
gical, doctrinal, ethical, social, and experiential dimensions
of religion - mysticism is a general name for religious experience together with part at least of the network of religious
practices which support it.
  I am emboldened to equate mysticism in this way with the
experiental core of religion by the fact that two of our practising mystics have said something very like this, whilst nothing
was said by the other three to suggest dissent. Brother David
defined mysticism as "experience of communion with the source
of meaning"; and he stressed that all who worship, and indeed
all who are conscious of the divine, are mystics. And Swami
Prabuddhananda defined mysticism as the realisation of relationship between the individual soul and the infinite reality, and

again, as being consciously in relation to God or to Brahman.
This would mean that all who are conscious of existing in the
presence of the divine are mystics. This would in turn mean,
in both cases, that rather than religious people being divided
into a small minority of mystics and a large majority of non-
mystics, we should equate mysticism with religious experience or
religious consciousness as such, but recognizing, of course,
many degrees of consciousness of the Transcendent, as well as
many forms which this consciousness can take.

Thus far it is not very clear why we need the term 'mysticism'
in addition to 'religious experience' and 'devotional practice'.
Nevertheless, we do have the word, and its use in the title of
this Conference is a sign of its continuing life. The word
clearly meets a need; and that need is, I think, two-fold.
There is first the inevitable distinction between what can be
variously called conventional, nominal, external or second-
hand religion on the one hand, and real, true, or first-hand
religion on the other. The former has always, in all large
traditions, been the major part of the total phenomenon of
religion. And it has seemed convenient, and perhaps reassur-
ing, to the mass of ordinary adherents of a religious traditon,
to whom their faith means conformity to the customary creed and
ritual of their society, to bestow a special label upon the
minority among them who live by a first-hand experience of the
Transcendent, with the implied suggestion that the latter
follow a special and peculiar way which is not for everyone.
And second, there is the fact that mysticism, in the broad sense
of what may be called first-hand religion as such, is continuous
with rare forms of religious experience which are reported by a
minority within the minority and which involve the paranormal or
supernatural, in the seeing of visions or the hearing of voices,
in yet rarer experiences of oneness with the Transcendent which
language can barely begin to express.

Any full theory of mysticism, or of religious experience, must
take account both of the kind of experiences reported by our
practising mystics and also of the rarer experiences of visions
and voices and of the unitive life to which the label
'mysticism' is sometimes restricted. However, I shall confine
myself here to the level or stage of religious experience
described by our three reporters, this constituting - as I pre-
sume - a stage on a spiritual journey which leads eventually to
the unitive life in God; or to Azilut, the highest world, in
which 'there is only One and no other and the soul is a moment
of God'; or is moksha; or nirvana.

II

Let us reserve for later the question, which is of course

ultimately all-important, whether it is reasonable for those who
experience life religiously to base their beliefs upon this
experience. For, as we must all be well aware in this sceptical age, it is always in principle possible to dismiss religious
experience as a fantasy or projection; and I shall in due course
come to this crucial issue. But for the moment let us bracket
off that question and assume that the several reports of the
mystics, and the wider traditions of belief out of which they
come, are substantially true. Let us assume that these are
substantially accurate accounts of experiences on the inter-
face between the human and the divine. What metaphysical
hypothesis, or picture of the universe, is implied in this
supposition? Any answer, within the confines of this paper, must
of course be in very large and general terms.

First, the Transcendent of which the mystics speak is of
the nature of mind rather than of matter; and accordingly a
distinction between matter, on the one hand, and spirit, soul,
mind or consciousness on the other, is implicit in a great deal
that they have said. The Transcendent, let us then say, is
infinite Spirit.

It follows, second, that the material universe is other than
the infinite Spirit, or at any rate other than the infinite
Spirit *per se*. Matter may (as the Semitic religions teach) be
wholly other than, and created out of nothing by, the infinite
Spirit, or (as the religions of Indian origin teach) it may be a
kind of illusion or dream experienced at some level of the
infinite Consciousness, or again it may be related to that
Consciousness somewhat as body to mind. But on any of these
views, matter is not simply identical with the infinite Spirit
as such. And because the material universe is thus either really
or illusorily other than the eternal Spirit, its real existence,
or its existence as a real illusion, is not self-explanatory.
Indeed, so far from being self-explanatory, its existence constitutes for us, who are parts of it, the ultimate mystery.
There seems to be a metaphysical analogue of Gödel's theorem,
to the effect that, from the point of view of a consciousness
which is part of the universe, any systematic interpretation
of the universe must generate at least one question which that
system can never answer. And for the religious systems it is
essentially the same question, though posed in different terms
within the different traditions. For the theistic religions it
is the question why a perfect and self-sufficient God has
created something other than, and of necessity inferior to, himself. For the non-theistic system of Advaita Vedanta it is the
question why the illusion of finite and material existence
occurs at all - for an illusion is just as truly something whose
occurrence demands an explanation as is a non-illusion: the
existence of the material world has not become any less problem-

43

atic when it has been labelled an illusion.   For non-theistic
Buddhism, the unanswerable question is why the wheel of *samsara*
turns.   (One has to define the problem as its turning rather
than its existing; for *samsara* is a process, consisting wholly
in a series of events.)   The immediate answer is that it turns
by the power of *tanhā* (craving, thirst, desire); but why is there
this apparently otiose phenomenon of finite consciousness and
its cravings?   This is the Buddhist form of the unanswerable
question which appears elsewhere as the questions why there is
maya and why there is a created universe.
There is, then, the mysterious fact of material existence.
And accepting it as a fact, we can see that, whether or not by
design, it has the effect of allowing a plurality of finite individuals existing over against one another.   We are distinct
beings because consciousness is exercised in us through separate
bodily organisms in virtue of which we are aware of the world
from particular positions within it.   Further, we are conscious
from the point of view of living organisms each programmed
for its own survival.   And whether we are parts or aspects of the
infinite Spirit, somehow separated from it (even though the
separation be an illusion of our finite consciousness) or are
real beings created *ex nihilo* by the infinite Spirit, we have in
either case a certain all-important affinity with that supreme
infinite Spirit.   And such conscious relationship, which
Schleiermacher called God-consciousness, and which more broadly
we can call consciousness of the Transcendent, is as it seems
to me, the essential religious or mystical experience.

III

What is the nature of our human consciousness of the Transcendent?
In the mysticism of our reporters, it occurs within the
context of this world, for they are men living on this earth.
And the epistemological character of this experience enjoyed by
the soul *in via* is not, I suggest, peculiar to religious consciousness.   On the contrary, what is going on is not fundamentally different in character from what is going on in other
forms of awareness which we take to be awareness of our environment.   For in all our conscious experiencing there is an important
element of cognitive choice, and this element in religious
awareness is continuous with the element of subjective interpretation in our other awarenesses.   I mean by this that when we
are aware of a thing (such as this pen) or aware of being in a
particular kind of situation (such as our present situation of
participating in a Conference) we are interpreting what is before

us, or around us, in terms of concepts. And by 'interpreting' here I do not mean the intellectual exercise of conscious theory-construction, as when we speak of the prosecution's interpretation of the evidence in a court of law, or , on a grander scale, of a philosopher's interpretation of the universe. I am referring to interpretation in the sense in which this enters continuously into our ordinary sense experience. For it is a commonplace today that in our ordinary everyday perception of our physical environment as having the character that we perceive it to have, the mind is constantly active - comparing, remembering, selecting, grouping, presuming, and, above all, recognizing - that is to say, being aware of our environment as having the particular character that we perceive (and of course often misperceive) it to have.

For example, I want to say that in seeing this biro pen, I am seeing what is before me *as* a biro - borrowing and extending the notion of 'seeing-as' which Wittgenstein discussed in the *Philosophical Investigations*. Wittgenstein himself thought that the notion only applies to special cases, like puzzle pictures: for example, you can see Jastrow's duck/rabbit *as* a picture of a duck or *as* a picture of a rabbit. But I want to say that *all* seeing-as, or more broadly that all conscious experiencing, is experiencing-as. That is to say, it involves *recognizing* objects and situations by means of concepts; or in other words, perceiving them as having this or that particular character or significance. For consider this biro. Surely, you might say, it is impossible to see it as anything other than a biro; and therefore the idea of seeing-*as*, implying as it does some sort of ambiguity in what is seen, is not appropriate. But to be conscious of seeing a biro, to be identifying *this* as a biro, is to be using a concept which has been created within a particular culture and which functions within certain cultures and not in others. We in North America and Europe see certain things as biro pens; but doubtless in rural Tibet they do not. And in Europe and North American a century ago they did not. Of course those who lack this concept could soon acquire it, and would then be able to see this as a biro pen. But the dispositional capacity to recognize it as such, to see it in this way, is not innate to the human mind but is on the contrary a cultural product. Again, to experience what is now going on as a seminar discussion presupposes a certain cultural background: beings from the planet Mars might well suppose something quite different to be taking place.

This second example, of being aware of the nature of a situation, is more to the point than the previous example of recognizing an individual object. For we are all the time within situations of various kinds, indeed usually within a number of

different situations at the same time - for example, the situation
of being in this room (on which our attention might become
focussed if someone were to shout out that there is a bomb
concealed in it); the situation of participating in a discussion
(on which our attention is I hope in fact concentrated); the
situation of being a Canadian or American or British citizen;
the situation of being father, mother, son or daughter, brother
or sister, or colleague; of being a human being over against
the mystery of existence; or - could it be? - the situation of
being in the presence of God, or of being part of the *samsaric*
process which leads to eventual oneness with the eternal
reality. And these are not mutually exclusive situations;
someone could be in all of them at once but with the spotlight
of his attention moving back and forth amongst them.

Let us speak, then, of our experiencing situations as having
this or that character, it being always the case that in order
so to experience we have to have a certain conceptual and interpretative equipment, often a very complex equipment. And one
feature of situational awareness to which I should like to
draw attention is that it involves tendencies or dispositions
to act in ways appropriate to the perceived character of the
situation. For one important thing about a situation in
which we find ourselves is that we are *in* it, part of it, and
have therefore to conduct ourselves in terms of its character
as we perceive it. The appropriate action may of course often
be inaction, or just going on doing the same thing. For example,
consciousness of our present situation as being the situation
of my reading a paper on a subject which we are all going to
discuss together involves, on my part, that I go on reading my
paper, and on your parts that you go on listening and preparing
points for the later discussion. Every form of situational
awareness has its own practical dispositional aspect. Thus, to
be conscious of being in a certain kind of situation is,
amongst other things, to be in a dispositional state to act
in this rather than in that way or range of ways. And this is
as true of religious as of secular cases. To be conscious of
living in the presence of the Transcendent has all kinds of
practical implications. For example, to be conscious of existing in the presence of God as Jesus depicted him, is not to be
anxious about the future, not to be afraid of other people but
on the contrary full of love for them all, and it is to believe
that whatever happens to one, one is in the divine presence
and within God's loving providence. Again, to be conscious of
being a 'spark of divinity', wrapped in illusion but struggling
towards the clear light of reality, is to be set upon overcoming one's own egoity and upon breaking the many threads of
selfish desire which hold one back.

I have been suggesting, then, that religious experience
exhibits a common structure, which it shares with all our other
cognitive experience, and that this is the experiencing of
situations in terms of certain concepts. And awareness of a
situation as having a certain character includes an appropriate
dispositional stance. We can call the experienced character
of a situation, in virtue of which we are in a certain dispositional state in relation to it, its meaning - or, more
precisely, the meaning that we have found in it. Meaning,
then, is the experienced character of a situation such that to
experience it as having that character is to be in a distinctive dispositional state in relation to it. And so we can
speak of the different meanings of human life - of the global
human situation - which different religious traditions enable
men to be aware of and to live in terms of.

IV

This diversity of religious meanings is brought out by comparing the reports of our practising mystics. If we assumed
that they were all deluded, the differences between their
delusions would not present any basic problem. But assuming,
as I am, that they are not deluded, one has to consider
whether the diversity of these experiences is compatible with
their all being experiences of the same transcendent reality.

Clearly, the possibility to be explored is that the concepts,
which we have seen to be involved in all experience, may
account for the same transcendent reality being experienced in
different ways.

Does Christian consciousness differ from Hindu, and Jewish
from Buddhist, because in these different traditions different
concepts of the Transcendent enter into the formation of one's
religious experience? And if so, how is it that the Transcendent is capable of being conceptualized in such different ways?

In order to answer these questions we need, I think, a
broadly Kantian epistemology.

There are, of course, many difficult and disputed questions
of Kantian interpretation. But the main outlines of his
epistemology are clear enough. He distinguished between the
noumenal world, which exists independently of man's perception
of it, and the phenomenal world, which is that world experienced
in terms of the various forms and categories that constitute
the structure of our human consciousness. All that we know
about the noumenal world is that it is the unknown reality
whose impact upon us produces the phenomenal world of conscious
experience. An analogous distinction has to be drawn, and
has indeed often been drawn, in man's thought of the

Transcendent. Perhaps its most explicit form is the Hindu distinction between *nirguna* Brahman, Brahman without attributes, beyond the scope of human language, and *saguna* Brahman, Brahman with attributes, known within human religious experience as Ishvara, the personal creator and governor of the Universe. In the west the Christian mystic Meister Eckhart distinguished between the Godhead (*Deitas*) and God *(Deus)*; and Rudolf Otto, in his comparative study of Eckhart and Shankara, says, 'Herein lies the most extraordinary analogy between Eckhart and Sankara: high above God and the personal Lord abides the "Godhead", having an almost identical relationship to God as that of Brahman to Isvara'- (*Mysticism East and West* p 14). More recently, Paul Tillich has spoken of the 'God above the God of theism' (*The Courage to Be* p 190) and has said that 'God is the symbol of God' (*Dynamics of Faith* p 46) Whitehead, and the process theologians who have followed him, distinguish between the primordial and the consequent natures of God, the former being his nature in himself, and the latter being formed by his response to and inclusion of the world. And Gordon Kaufman distinguishes between the 'real God' and the 'available God', the former being an 'utterly unknowable X', and the latter 'essentially a mental or imaginative construction' (*God the Problem* p 86). A more traditional form of the distinction is that between God in himself, in his infinite self-existent being, beyond the grasp of the human mind, and God in relation to mankind, revealed as creator and redeemer. In one form or another the distinction seems unavoidable for any view which is not willing to reduce God to a finite being who can, in principle, be wholly known by the human mind and defined within human concepts. If God is infinite, he must pass out into sheer mystery beyond the reach of our knowledge and comprehension, and in his limitless transcendence he is *nirguna*, ultimate Godhead, the God above the God of theism.

But if we see such concepts as *nirguna* Brahman, the Godhead, and the God above God, as pointing to the unknowable divine noumenon, we need not necessarily follow the advaitist Hindu thinkers in equating the divine noumenon with impersonal reality, in contrast to personal deities who are merely phenomenal. The personalist-dualist experience of I-Thou encounter between a human self and the transcendent Self, and the monistic or advaitic consciousness of one-ness with infinite non-personal being, are alike experiences of divine phenomena. All that we can say of the divine noumenon is that it is the source and ground of all those experienced realities, as also of human minds in their awareness of these different phenomenal forms.

The thesis we are considering, then, is that religious experience is experience of the Transcendent, not however as

divine noumenon but as divine phenomenon. The Transcendent
as phenomenal object of man's religious experience is a
joint product of the divine noumenon itself and the various
human concepts of the Transcendent which have developed within
different human cultures. These concepts have a common source
in man's innate religiousness - that is, in our tendency to
experience religiously, or in terms of the Transcendent; and
the specific forms taken by the generic concept of the Transcendent arise from the manifold influences which have produced
the varied ways of thinking and feeling that are characteristic of different human cultures.

But why are there these different human concepts of the
Transcendent, correlated with different forms of religious
awareness, different kinds of cult, and different ways of living
and worshipping? To answer this question in detail is the task
of the historians, anthropologists and sociologists of religion,
and is a task which they may or may not ever be able fully to
discharge. But the general conclusion seems inevitable that
concepts of the Transcendent are related to the conditions of
human life in different ages and different parts of the world -
in short, to different human cultures.

As earnest of more fully developed theories for which we may
hope in the future, such suggestions as the following have been
made: 'In nomadic, pastoral, herd-keeping societies, the male
principle predominates; among agricultural peoples, aware of
the fertile earth which brings forth from itself and nourishes
its progency upon its broad bosom, it is the mother principle
which seems important. Among Semitic peoples therefore, whose
traditions are those of herdsmen, the sacred is thought of in
male terms: God the father. Among Indian peoples whose
traditions has been for many centuries, and even millenia,
agricultural, it is in female terms that the sacred is understood: God the mother.' (Trevor Ling, *Religion East and West*
p 27).

I am not equipped either to criticise or to contribute to this
work of relating the several kinds of religious experience and
thought to the different circumstances of man's life. But it
seems clear that, whether or not we can successfully trace
them, all manner of environing influences have gone into the
formation of the different human cultures; and that many of
these same influences must have affected the religions which
are aspects, and indeed usually central aspects, of those
cultures. And once a broad cultural stream is flowing, even the
new revelatory experiences and insights of the great spirits who
arise within it are bound to share the basic character of that
stream. Thus, it is not surprising that Gautama the Buddha
lived in India and Jesus the Christ in Palestine.

There is a very important difference to be noted between our

awareness of the Transcendent and our awareness of our material
environment, with our awareness of other human selves standing
somewhere between these extreme cases. This is a difference
within the dimension which has been thought of as the degrees
of value and also as the degrees of reality or being - although in the Platonic tradition these two scales were identified as one. When we add that it is of the essence of human
existence - whether as child of God or as divine spark - to be
finitely free, we see that our relationship to that which is
superior to ourselves in value or in fullness of being will
differ in character from our relationship to that which is
inferior to ourselves, with our relationship to that which is
on the same level as ourselves falling between these two
extremes. We are not diminished in our essential dignity or
freedom by being aware of the existence of realities below ourselves in the scale of value or of reality. The power of storm
and earthquake, or the strength of elephant or tiger, dwarfs
my own strength; and the vastness of the universe around us
shows us by comparison as microscopically small. But man
nevertheless transcends the whole world of nature, with all
its immensity of power, by his consciousness of it; as Pascal
said, 'if the universe were to crush him, man would still be
more noble than that which killed him, because he knows that
he dies and the advantage which the universe has over him; the
universe knows nothing of this' (*Pensées* no 347). And in relation to other human beings, whilst many are more successful,
or more intelligent, or more wealthy, or more powerful, etc.,
yet they are still in the end only fellow mortals and thus
ultimately on the same level as myself. But in relation to
absolute value or absolute reality I am nothing, and can have
no personal being and freedom in relation to it, unless the
infinitely good reality allows me largely to shut it out of my
consciousness. Accordingly, we preserve our freedom over against
that which is infinitely superior to ourselves by being aware
of it, not in its infinite fullness, but in terms of limited
and limiting concepts.

In theistic terms, to be directly confronted by infinite
goodness and love, infinite knowledge and power, infinite
fullness of being and life, would deprive us of any independence.
There would be no room for a free human response of faith and
love, or of trust and obedience. Indeed, the disparity between
our finite selves and the infinite divine reality would exclude
our very existence as relatively autonomous centres of finite
freedom. Therefore God has to be the hidden God, veiling himself
by creating us at an epistemic distance in order that he may then
progressively reveal himself to us in limited ways which respect
and preserve our own human freedom as persons. Again, in

50

non-theistic terms, it is the finite individual's relative ignorance (*avidya*) of Brahman that constitutes his own finite individuality. As he rightly exercises his freedom through the long process of *samsara*, separate individuality is eventually transcended and he becomes the infinite Spirit. (Why, in view of this, there should be finite centres of freedom at all is the ultimate mystery that we noted earlier as fulfilling the metaphysical analogue of Gödel's theorem).

It has been suggested, for example by Bergson, that one function of the brain is to filter out the virtual infinity of information reaching us through our senses, so that what comes to consciousness is the relatively simple and manageable world which we perceive and can successfully inhabit. We also have a system for filtering out the Transcendent and reducing it to forms with which we can cope; for 'human kind cannot bear very much reality'. This system is religion, which is our resistance (in the electronic sense) to the infinite Transcendent. In the earliest stages of man's development, the Transcendent was reduced in human awareness to the dimensions of man's own image, so that the gods were, like human kings, often cruel and bloodthirsty; or to the dimensions of the tribe or nation, as the symbol of its unity and power; or again to the more ample dimensions of the forces of nature, such as the life-giving and yet burning radiance of the sun, or the destructive power of storm and earthquake, or the mysterious pervasive force of fertility. And the response that was required, the way of life which such awareness rendered appropriate, was a communal response. For the anthropologists have shown us how closely knit primitive societies have been, and how little scope they offered for individual thought, whether in religion or in other aspects of life. As Robertson Smith wrote long ago, 'Religion in primitive times was not a system of belief with practical applications: it was a body of fixed traditional practices, to which every member of society conformed as a matter of course'. (*The Religion of the Semites* 3rd ed. p. 20) It was with the gradual emergence of individuality, in what Jaspers has called the axial period, particularly during the second half of the first millenium B.C., that higher conceptions of the Transcendent developed in correlation with a deeper sense of moral claim upon human life, and upon the individual as well as the collectivity.

For it was the emergence of the individual, and in particular of the religious individual, that made possible those great souls or *mahatmas* on whose consciousness the Transcendent impinged in new ways or with new intensity and power. The greatest of these became founders of religious traditions – Moses, Zoroaster, Confucius, Gautama, Jesus, and later Mohammad.

Others effected important developments within existing traditions - the Hebrew prophets, the writers of the Upanishads
and of the Bhagavad Gita, Pythagoras, Socrates, Plato. Each of
the great religious traditions has of course continued to develop
in larger and smaller ways through the centuries, one form each
of contemporary Buddhism, Christianity, Hinduism, and Judaism
being represented in the material prepared for this Conference.
    The broad hypothesis which I am suggesting, then, is that
the infinite Spirit presses in all the time upon the multiplicity of finite human spirits, and yet always so that our
finite awareness of this encompassing reality is filtered
through a set of human religious concepts. When the developing
human race produces a spirit who is able to respond to the
Transcendent in a new and fuller way, his (or her) experience
of the Transcendent overflows or breaks the system of religious
concepts inherited from his culture, and he proclaims a new
truth about God or about the meaning of the process of existence,
bringing with it new demands for the living of human life.

V

    All this is hypothesis, of the kind which we are led to
develop when we accept as true the religious-experience reports
of the mystics. But can we, and indeed can they, properly
have confidence in those reports? Let us, in this last
section, consider the question of the cognitive value of
religious experience.
    The central feature of the mystics' reports is that they speak
of a divine reality other than the human mind and other than
the material universe which is our present environment. This
transcendent reality is experienced as the God of the theistic
religions and as Brahman or the Void in the non-theistic
religions; and I have suggested that these are all divine
phenomena constituting forms in which the unknown divine
noumenon impinges upon human consciousness. The status of
these divine phenomena (which I am generically calling the
Transcendent) is thus comparable with that of the phenomenal
world in Kant's critical philosophy. That world exists independently of the individual human consciousness, being common
to a community of minds functioning in the same way - this
community being, in the case of the phenomenal world, co-
extensive with the human race. But the perceived world, although thus objectively real in relation to ourselves, is still
a phenomenon constituting the particular way in which the
noumenal reality becomes the object of our finite human
consciousness. In an analogous way, God, Yahweh, Allah,
Brahman, the Void, in so far as these are objects of man's

religious experience, are divine phenomena constituting ways
in which the unknown divine noumenon impinges upon human
consciousness within different religious communities, with
their different concepts of the Transcendent.

Our question now concerns the reality, over against our human
consciousness, of God, Brahman, and the other divine phenomena.
Can we properly claim to know that God exists, or that Brahman
is real?

We must be careful to pose the question rightly. Whenever
we ask whether x exists - whether x be an electron, a tree, a
house, a human consciousness, or Brahman, or God - we must
not exclude ourselves, as the cognising minds asking the
question, from the picture. The apparently purely objective
question, Does x exist? is always in reality the objective/
subjective question, Do I know that x exists; Is the existence
of x an item of knowledge, i.e. of my knowledge? But even
this reformulation is not yet quite right. For most philosophers prefer to define knowledge in ideal terms so that 'I
know p' entails p, and there can thus be no knowing p except
when p is in fact the case. This ideal definition has many
advantages, but it also has the inconvenience that we are never
entitled to certify definitely that we know, but only to
register claims to know. We can claim to know that p i.e.,
claim that what we present as our well warranted belief that
p corresponds with the facts. But this claim must necessarily
be made from the perspective of our own finite range of data.
And it is not open to us, having made that claim from our own
particular and limited standpoint, to go on to certify it from
an unlimited or ideal perspective. Only omniscience could know
that a human being's claimed knowledge is indeed knowledge
in the ideal sense. We have the data on the basis of which we
claim to have knowledge, but we do not have further data, or
knowledge that there are no further data, such as only
omniscience could have. And therefore if we are to speak
strictly, we must speak not of $knowledge$ that the Transcendent
exists, but of a well-grounded knowledge claim. This is the
same as a well-grounded belief that the Transcendent exists;
and I shall accordingly speak interchangeably of well-grounded
beliefs and well-grounded knowledge claims. Our question is
thus not properly formulated as 'whether the Transcendent exists'
but 'whether there is well-grounded human belief that the
Transcendent exists'.

At this point we turn to the mystics, and above all to the
great souls whose religious experience lies at the origin of
the major world faiths. I shall put the argument in terms of
the theistic experience of living in the presence of God; but
a parallel argument will apply to the non-theistic forms of
religious experience. In the theistic world, then, such a

person as Jesus was as powerfully conscious of being in the presence of God as he was of the presence of other human beings and of his physical environment. And so let us ask: is it rational for such a person, experiencing in this way, to believe and to claim to know, on the basis of his own experience, that God is real?

I suggest that it *is* rational for him to make such a claim, and indeed that it would be irrational on his part not to. We have to trust our own experience for otherwise we have no basis on which to believe anything about the nature of the universe in which we find ourselves. Of course we also know that sometimes particular parts of our experience are delusory, so that experience is not *always* to be trusted. But we only know this on the basis of trust in the general veracity of our experience. We cannot go beyond our experience as a whole; for there is no 'beyond' for us to go to, since any further data that we may come to have must, when we have it, form part of our experience as a whole. And if some aspect of our experience is sufficiently intrusive and persistent, and coherent with the rest of our experience, then to reject it would be in effect to doubt our own sanity and would thus amount to a kind of cognitive suicide. One who has a powerful and continuous sense of existing in the presence of God *must*, as a rational person, claim to know that God exists; and he is as entitled to make this claim as he and the rest of us are to claim to know that the physical world exists and that other people exist. In each case doubt is theoretically possible: a solipsism which reduces the world, or other minds, or God, to a modification of one's own private consciousness remains a logical possibility. But we are so made that we live, and can only live, on the basis of our experience and on the assumption that it is generally cognitive of reality transcending our own consciousness. Indeed, what we call sanity consists in acting on the basis of our putatively cognitive experience as a whole. And this being so, the religious man, experiencing life in terms of the presence of God, is rationally entitled to believe what he experiences to be the case - namely that God is real, or exists.

But having said this one must immediately add certain qualifications. For we cannot say that *all* religious and quasi-religious experiences, without exception, provide a good grounding for knowledge-claims. Just as there are illusions and delusions in other fields of experience, so also in religious experience. Suppose, for example, someone experiences his life in terms of witchcraft, or astrology, or alchemy, or influences from extra-galactic intelligences who visit this earth in flying saucers, or in some other way which most of us regard as perverse or crazy. What are we to say about such a form of experience?

Let us suppose that the person concerned makes a knowledge-claim on the basis of his experience. Are we to hold that he is rationally entitled to make such a claim? The question, I would suggest, becomes the question whether we regard him as a fully sane, sober and rational person. If we do so regard him, we must also regard him as entitled to trust his own experience and to base knowledge-claims upon it. And our judgment as to whether he is fully sane, sober and rational will have two dimensions. One will be our estimate of the person himself; and here our assessment is partly psychological and partly moral. The criteria for such judgments are of course very hard to formulate; and yet it is clear that we are accustomed to make judgments in this area almost every day of our lives. The other dimension concerns the content of the knowledge-claim. It can only be rational to base a knowledge-claim upon some aspect of our experience if that claim is consistent with our other knowledge, based as this is upon the rest of our experience. And it may well be that knowledge-claims about the truth of witchcraft, or astrology, or alchemy, or about the existence of extra-galactic intelligences who visit the earth in flying saucers, fail to cohere with what we know on the basis of our experience as a whole. In particular, such claims may clash with our scientific knowledge. In that case the wider experience will, in a rational person, provide a context within which the special experience is criticized, and bracketed as peculiar and suspect. And when, in hearing reports of astrological or other eccentric experience-reports, we judge the beliefs based upon such experience to be incompatible with public scientific knowledge, we shall probably hold that the person holding the belief is irrational or eccentric and that his special form of experience is not to be relied upon. For it is only if we can accept both that his special beliefs *may* be true and that he is a sane and well-balanced human being, that we feel obliged to take his experience-reports seriously.

How does all this apply to the religious case? It means that a rational person will only trust his own religious experience, and will only trust the religious experience reports of others, if the beliefs to which they give rise are beliefs which he judges *may* be true. In the theistic case, the existence of God must be judged to be possible if the 'experience of living in God's presence' is to be taken seriously. This is where rational theology, or natural theology, comes into its own. Its office, I would suggest, is not to prove that God exists, or even that God's existence is probable; but to establish the possibility of divine existence. Without arguing the matter here I believe that reason can ascertain that it is *possible*

that there is a God; and in that case theistic religious-
experience has to be taken seriously. But whether experiences
in terms of witchcraft, astrology, alchemy, flying saucers,
etc., are to be taken seriously depends upon a corresponding
rational scrutiny of the content of the knowledge-claims to
which they give rise.

The final question that I must briefly raise is this: suppose,
for the sake of argument, we accept the right of the great
theistic mystics to believe in the reality of God on the basis
of their own religious experience. We shall then be prepared
to acknowledge that such a person as Jesus or St. Paul or St.
Francis or Martin Luther, or again Mohammad, or Ramanuja, or
Guru Nanak, have been entitled, as rational persons, to claim
on the basis of their own experiences to know that God exists.
But what about ordinary religious believers, who do not enjoy
the same overwhelmingly powerful forms of theistic experience?
Does our line of thought point to any justification for belief
in the existence of God (or the reality of Brahman) on the part
of ordinary people? Not, I would say, if they do not experience
religiously in any degree whatever. For the absolutely un-
mystical - if such there are - there can be no good grounds for
religious belief. However, the ordinary believer does, I would
think, have some at least remote echo within his own experience
of the much more momentous experience of the great religious
figures. And it is this that makes him take their reports
seriously. If he experiences his own life religiously at least
to some slight extent, this makes it possible, and I would
suggest reasonable, for him to be so impressed by the reports
of the great souls that he comes to share their belief in the
reality of the Transcendent. His belief is not *as* well-
grounded as theirs is. But I would suggest that it is well
enough grounded for it to be reasonable for him to proceed in
faith in the footsteps of a religious leader, anticipating the
full confirmation which his faith will ultimately receive if it
does indeed correspond with reality.

Reflection on Professor John Hick's
"Mystical Experience as Cognition"
By JOHN HEINTZ

Professor Hick's paper raises a number of important points in a
provocative way. They are subject to both philosophic and religious criticisms, although it is easier to grasp the latter once
one has seen the former.

Professor Hick's paper, as he read it to the conference, falls
into three major parts. The first is an affirmation: religious
experience is the core of religion, and mystical experience differs
only in degree (a very high degree) from the sort of experience
shared by most participants in organized religions. The explanatory aspect of religion is secondary. In the second part of his
paper he employs the language of Kant to present a picture of the
real world as noumenal, the world of experience as phenomenal. In
a familiar way, due to Wittgenstein and his followers, all experience is pictured as interpreted. To see an object is to see it
as this or that, a ball-point pen or a toy, perhaps. To experience anything is, necessarily, to experience it as falling
under some concept. The mystics' descriptions of their experiences are then, according to Professor Hick, all experiences of
the noumenal, transcendent, unqualified godhead (or "god above
god" in Tillich's phrase), experienced phenomenally and exper-
ienced-as (interpreted as) falling under one or another concept
according to the mystics' different traditions.

Professor Hick then argues, in his third main section, that it
is rational for a mystic to accept his experiences as veridical,
that is, as experiences of an existent god, provided that they
cohere intelligibly with the remainder of his own and others'
experiences (including such scientific beliefs as are warranted
by those experiences.) So a religious adherent who has reason
to believe that the great soul who founded his religion was
sincere, and who knows enough of that person's experiences, will
have reason to believe that the founder did really experience an
existing god, with the attributes accorded that god in the religious tradition.

Professor Hick has not in fact shown that it is irrational for a
great soul to doubt that his experience gives him a well-grounded
belief that god is real. Hick can give a schematic account of a
case in which the experience would ground such a knowledge claim,
but only, I will try to show, by granting the explanatory aspect of
religion a more important role. Suppose a great soul has such an
intense, powerful, coherent experience that he cannot but believe
that it was an experience of an existing god. Suppose too, however, that he is prepared to consider the question (not so far as

57

to actually doubt) whether the experience gives good grounds for his belief.[1]

To ask this question at all is for the mystic to treat his experience as a phenomenon (an experiencing-as) as one of his non-mystic followers would, accepting his master's sincerity, treat the master's report as the report of a certain experience. The question cannot arise at all if the experience is simply formulated as "experiencing the transcendent as...." Such a formulation just begs the question. I am appealing to a clear standard case of Professor Hick's, namely, seeing what is in my hand *as* a ball-point pen. In seriously asking the question whether my visual experience properly grounds my belief that what is in my hand *is* a ball-point pen, I can hardly describe my experience as "seeing the ball-point pen in my hand as a pen". I might describe the experience in neutral ways, or explicitly withhold the commitment to truth: "It was the sort of experience one has when one is looking at a ball-point pen in one's hand."

The difference between experience grounding a belief in a ball-point pen and the experience grounding a belief in the existence of a transcendent god is that the former is both more familiar and more widely shared than the latter.[2] The mystic and his follower alike will entertain, in the latter case, hypotheses of drug-induced state, hallucination, yogic ecstasy, perhaps even (temporary, partial) insanity. A fully sane, sober, rational person may on occasion doubt that a given experience was an experience of what it seemed to be, and all the more so if the object is, or is supposed to be, a person or a person's mental state. "Was he deceiving me or himself?" we sometimes ask, and do not know the answer right off.

As Hick points out, for the experience of something as ϕ to be veridical, it must be possible for that thing to be ϕ. It must be consistent with all we know. Asking whether something's being ϕ is consistent with all we know is part of asking whether its being ϕ is the best explanation of our having experienced it *as* ϕ, in the context of everything else we know. That this in my hand which I see *as* a ball-point pen *is* a ball-point pen is the best explanation in these circumstances for my having the visual experience I now have, having certain tactile experiences, experiencing the words flow across the page, and so on. Another explanation, even if possible, is ruled out if it is less plausible.[3] If, in the mystic's case, there happens to be a better explanation for his experience than that he was, for example, in the presence of god, then it is rational for him -- and therefore us -- to doubt whether he was in the presence of god.

Professor Hick objects to this account of the rationality of a mystic's doubt at least partly because, when the mystic comes to believe that he is in the presence of god, he is not first exam-

ining his experience, then forming his belief as its best explanation. This is a red herring. Hick has already asked us to accept
that *all* experience is experiencing-as, and is thus theory-laden,
influenced by our knowledge, expectations, situation and science.
We do not, of course, experience first, then interpret. If we did,
the first experience would not be experiencing-as. It is in the
context of justifying our claim that what we experience *as* a ball-
point pen *is* a ball-point pen, that it is appropriate to ask
whether that is the best explanation. And it is in the context of
justifying a mystic's claim that what he experienced *as* being in
the presence of god *was* being in the presence of god, that it is
appropriate, indeed necessary, for him to ask whether that is the
best explanation.

So far, I follow Hick in treating alike the experiences of something *as* a ball-point pen and of something *as* being in the presence of god. But they differ in a way that makes life harder for
the adherents of religion. 'Being in the presence of god', 'being
in union with the one', 'nothing', 'a blinding light', are ways in
which great souls have described their experiences of what Hick
identifies as the unqualified, transcendent godhead. These descriptions are literally inconsistent with one another, as 'long,
green, shiny object', 'ball-point pen' are *not* inconsistent as
applied to experiences of this ball-point pen. (In this Professor
Hick seems to agree.) To accept the mystics' reports as *true*,
therefore, we are required to ignore the differences among them;
we are required to ignore the fact that one "experiences the transcendent" *as* being embraced by Christ, the resurrected son of God,
while another "experiences the transcendent" as nothing. What is
"true in common" to all mystics' experiences is therefore only a
minimal residue of the meaning of the mystics' descriptions. How
is it possible for the non-great soul to accept the teachings of
his faith as being confirmed by the founder's mystical experience,
if the claim grounded in that experience must be purged of all, or
almost all, its literal content? Quakers and Zen Buddhists may do
all right in this way -- their doctrinal claims are few -- but
pity the poor fundamentalist, the Scotch Presbyterian, the low-
church Anglican, the native American Indian, the Hindu and the
Hebrew student. Our claims about the material world (ball-point
pens) are validated by and asserted in the language of the phenomenal. According to Hick, our claims about the transcendent are
validated by the phenomenal, but *not* asserted in that limiting
language. The meaning of great mystical experience thus once
again eludes our normal canons for justification and belief.

FOOTNOTES

1   Recall that Swami Prabuddhananda remarked that much of the
     non-mystic yoga's experience is *just like* a mystical experi-
     ence. A great soul might acknowledge this and so entertain
     the question of veracity.

2   Hick indeed says that Kant's material phenomenal world is co-
     extensive with the human race, the same for all humans, but
     this is too strong. If all experience is, as he says,
     experiencing-as, then the experience of a person who is famil-
     iar with ball-point pens will on occasion differ from that of
     someone who does not know what they are. Their phenomenal
     worlds may overlap, but not entirely.

3   In reply to a question of Professor Horne, Professor Hick
     claimed that Solipsism was a simpler explanation of our expe-
     riences in the meeting room than was our belief that we were
     there with other people. This is a disingenuous remark, be-
     cause, since Strawson's *Individuals*, we know there are, at the
     least, real problems in even coherently formulating Solipsism.
     More important, this "simpler" explanation is not better,
     according to those who hold the "best explanation" view, for
     it fails to account for the many aspects of our experiences in
     the room which, like Professor Hick's talk itself, were not in
     the experiencers' power nor apparently in their power to imag-
     ine. Solipsism leaves quite a lot to be explained.

Response to Professor John Heintz
By JOHN HICK

I don't want to say — though I evidently gave the impression that
I did — that the notion of experiencing-as is meant to bridge the
gap between the Kantian noumenon and phenomenon, so that the
religious person experiences the divine noumenon *as* a divine
phenomenon. The experiencing-as of which I was speaking occurs
entirely within the phenomenal or experienced realm. That which
is experienced religiously by one person and non-religiously
by another is the world or, better, the process of human life.
The distinctively theistic experience is the experience of living
in this world in the unseen presence of God.

Given that the great theistic figures have experienced their
lives as being lived in God's presence, it is — as Heintz argues —
still possible to question whether they are justified in living
and believing on the basis of that experience. Even though the
religious man himself does not normally, whilst proceeding on
the basis of his distinctive religious experience, question his
own right to do so, yet this right can be questioned; and the
correct verdict concerning this claimed right should (as Heintz
says) be the same for the religious as for the non-religious
person. Here I have argued that, if the proposition believed
is intrinsically believable, the appropriate form of experience
constitutes a proper ground for believing it. And by the
appropriate form of experience I do not mean some momentary
episode, but a way of experiencing-as which is so long-lived,
coherent, and vivid that the experiencer cannot but take it to
be cognitive of reality.

When we apply this argument, as we must, not only to the
rationality of Christian belief but also to the rationality of
Jewish and Muslim, and again of Hindu and Buddhist belief, the
Kantian model suggests itself. We then postulate a divine
noumenon which becomes the object of human phenomenal experience
in a variety of forms, the differences between these different
divine phenomena being due to the varying human contributions to
these different awarenesses of the divine. So long as we
appreciate the phenomenal nature of the experienced divine, we
need not conclude that religious people in the different religious traditions, with their different doctrines arising out of
their different forms of experience, must be contradicting one
another. They may be enjoying varying — and perhaps even
varyingly adequate — experiences of the same divine noumenon.

The Exploration of Mysticism
By NINIAN SMART

The logic of the conference reflects types of reasons which people
have for being concerned about mysticism at the present time.
Perhaps I can expatiate on this before coming to comment upon what
two of our practitioners have written.

The period since World War II has been religiously of great significance. Partly because of culture-contacts arising from the
war itself, and in particular the American involvement with Japan;
partly because of a new awareness of the power of non-European
cultures during a period of decolonization; partly because of the
work of comparative religionists in interpreting and making available the spiritual traditions of the non-European world -- for
such reasons, Westerners were ready for an awakening of concern
for religions. This readiness also related to the alienation of
many from the orthodox Christian traditions. Official religion in
the West to some extent tried to cope by developing a new secular
theology; but it is doubtful whether such a new Christian humanism
and its passion for taking much of the religion out of the faith
could be very stable. In any event, as the counter culture movements of the late 60's were to show, there was a real drive for a
renewal of inner religion -- even if sometimes that drive should
express itself somewhat naively, through the use of LSD for example. But a great part of the interest in Eastern religions was
because they were perceived as having developed important methods
of contemplation, such as Zen meditation, Hindu and Buddhist yoga,
and so on. Even now, despite some advance by *bhakti* forms of
Hinduism in the West, such as the Hare Krishna movement, the main
interest probably remains in mysticism, i.e. inner-directed contemplative techniques of various kinds, and their attendant doctrines. So there has been a growth in the exploration of the more
familiar faiths of the Semitic group -- Sufism, the Kabbalah and
Christian contemplation attract new and lively concern. So the
first general point I wish to make about religion, in Western societies at least, is that the last decade has seen a remarkable
growth of interest in forms of meditation, often of Eastern prov-
enance.

In the main this interest has been practical, though it also has
generated some intellectual tendencies. It has been practical because modern society poses some acute practical questions, especially to those for whom the immediate needs of food, shelter and
so on are well, indeed abundantly, provided for. Some of these
questions concern the very work ethic which made modern industrial
society possible. The pursuit of contemplation, one aspect of the

63

hippie life-style, is a protest against an instrumental view of
things and persons. The perversions of technology also stimulate
a certain tendency to quietism, particularly evident, of course,
during the period of the Vietnam war. But most of all, there has
been a quest for psychological peace in a period of upheaval and
of the atomisation of society, and therefore a renewal of the
quest for a spiritual life based less on dogma and conformity than
upon inner experience.

This points to an important motif in the intellectual position
of many involved in this contemplative, orientalising movement.
It is the thought that there is somehow a single truth open to the
mystic transcending the particularities of the various outer traditions. In one form it is the Perennial Philosophy: in another
the flavour of Alan Watts. Nevertheless, even if there may be
alienation from the exclusivism of much Christian preaching, questions about the nature of the truth to be discussed remain.

This is where the counterculture and other movements I have
sketched so briefly abut upon philosophy. It happens that one
major interest among philosophers of religion has not unnaturally
been the question of the validity of religious experience: one
thinks of the writings of I.T. Ramsey, H.D. Lewis, Nelson Pike
and, earlier, W.T. Stace. Within the Wittgensteinian tradition,
the debate about "seeing-as" has a relation to the problem of
whether one can base belief somehow on experience. Of course, it
has been unfortunate that a number of prominent writings in the
field have failed to take due account of varieties of religions
and of religious experience (the debates very often take place
around a version of Western theism). Still there is now assuredly
a strong philosophical concern with problems about how claims
about religious experience, and within that of mysticism, should
be evaluated.

Of course, it could be argued that the spiritual consequences of
a type of mysticism do not result from the truth of the doctrines
used to interpret that form of mysticism. What gives peace gives
peace. So it is not necessary to hold to (for example) yoga theory to practice yoga; nor to believe in the Buddhist Dharma to be
elevated by Buddhist forms of meditation. In brief, it may be
that the philosophical questions about truth are irrelevant to the
practical quest. However, this thesis runs counter both to fact
and to conceptual analysis. For men wish to understand their situation . If something profound comes from the practice of mysticism then how is it so? We might discount God, Brahman or some
other transcendental source of this experience which is felt to be
profound: in that case there is some natural aspect of human life
-- the mind and the organism -- which yoga exploits. But that is
itself a theory. It is clear, then, that men wish to 'place'
their mysticism, and to give themselves some conceptual under-

standing of it.

Hence, there is a certain solidarity between the practical and more theoretical aspects of the exploration of mysticism. However, it should be said that there is a third world lying between that of the practising mystic and the philosopher, namely the world of empirical investigation. Of course, there are overlaps. After all, introspection is a form of investigation, while conceptual questions all the time arise in regard to the empirical appraisal of different kinds of mystical experience and contemplative techniques. Still, roughly we can make the threefold distinction. And what then do I mean by empirical investigation?

There is a range of enquiries which though relevant to philosophy and indeed to practical mysticism, are descriptive and/or explanatory in intent, and which rely on what may be called, roughly speaking, scientific methods. For example, there are the following: the investigation of changes in brain states, rhythms of breathing, etc., during yogic meditation; the attempt to find out as objectively as possible the similarities and dissimilarities between the experiences of different contemplatives in the same culture and between those in one culture and those in another, and the exploration of any relationship between personality types and adeptness in meditation; the investigation of drug experiences and their supposed likeness to mystical experiences; the historical study of famous mystics and mystical movements; the exploration of the social dimension of mysticism and why it appears to flourish more in one epoch or milieu than another, even within the same religious tradition -- and so on.

Such empirical investigations belong crudely to what we might call the scientific study of religion. By contrast, being a mystic belongs to the practical exploration of religion. Philosophical investigations concern the conceptual and truth-related problems of how to evaluate what scientific and practical explorations reveal. As I have said, the three aspects of the exploration of religion are interrelated, but the theoretical distinction between the three is important, in my view.

It so happens that a prime issue regarding what mystics say has both profound significance in the philosophy of religion and in what I have called the scientific study of religion. It has to do with the degree to which mystics interpret both their life and their experiences in terms of doctrinal presuppositions. There is of course no reason at all why they should not do so. If they belong to a tradition they doubtless should be loyal to it; and no doubt too they also wish to 'place' what happens to them and what they do in the wider perspective of a doctrinal or metaphysical scheme. Nevertheless, problems are presented when we try to compare what happens to a mystic in tradition Tl with what happens to one in T2. If the assumptions of Tl are very different from those

of T2 then probably the approach of a mystic in T1 will often
differ from the approach of one in T2 -- but also descriptions of
what may well be similar experiences will vary interpretatively.
But we should not be put off too much by such problems, but try to
probe behind the descriptions and assumptions. Let me give you an
earthier analogy. A person making love to his wife may differ in
attitude and description from another man making love with a pros-
titute: the significance of the two acts can be divergent, but
still the two acts of love involve copulation and a certain kind
of pleasurable experience (hopefully).

Let me consider then first what Swami Prabuddhananda writes. I
do not for a moment doubt the reality of what he says -- that is,
he speaks within a milieu and from a practice which has real consequences for the person who follows the path in question. Still,
there are problems.

First, his Vedantism is evident, and his interpretation of the
religious life stems from his account of the relationship between
the soul and God. These are entities realised in experience, but
not in utter nakedness do they come but trailing clouds of doctrine too.

Second, he rightly (in my view) holds that anyone can be a mystic. Yet also he appeals to scriptures -- they are 'an important
factor in a spiritual searcher's life'. It may well be. But some
cultures have scriptures which do not perhaps much conduce to mysticism, and some have no scriptures at all. It seems to me that
the very idea that authority or illumination should reside in a
body of literature (if that is the way to put it) is rather
strange. Also, how does one determine what scriptures one should
reflect on? I personally find the Pali Canon and the New Testa-
ment full of verve and meaning. But I can see others who find the
Upanishads or the Koran more dramatic and illuminating. However,
in all this I do not wish to criticise Swami Prabuddhananda's
standpoint so much as to raise the issue of tradition. Very often
mystics come out of and rely upon, traditions, part of which are
expressed in scriptures. But why does one need a tradition? After all, transcendental meditation is presented in effect as a
method for everyone, outside history, outside allegiances.

One main point, however, arising from the Swami's presentation
interests me strongly. He stresses that various practices, which
can easily exist outside the context of mysticism and the contemplative life, are useful thereto. Thus he lists among other
things pilgrimage, formal external worship and celebrations of the
birthdays of saints and spiritual teachers.

Now some of these things involve rituals which have no *necessary*
connection with the contemplative life, as I understand it. How
then do the rituals help? It could be that the case is similar to
work in much of the Christian monastic tradition -- the work is

predicated upon the slogan *laborare est orare*, and such work is a way of helping men to concentrate. And it could easily be that *religious* works such as pilgrimage have the same effect. However the Swami may be saying more -- that somehow God's grace is easier to come by in these situations. I am not decrying it; but what about a religion which has no grace, such as Theravada Buddhism? There too there are festivals, pilgrimages and the like, but not the idea of God's grace (rather the idea of the accumulation of merit).

But clearly such claims about the helpfulness of certain practices must be open to empirical check to some extent. Such investigations could well show correlations even if they left on one side the existence of God or of the eternal soul or of the identity or non-identity of the two supposed entities.

In brief it seems these are questions arising about Swami Prabuddhananda's presentation: one question concerns his use of doctrinal terms, in his general espousal of a certain form of Vedanta, and the second has to do with how he sees the relationship between worship and ritual on the one hand and inner contemplation on the other.

Perhaps I can briefly turn aside here to put forward what I see as the pattern in various religions and phases of religion. Necessarily the picture I draw is a crude one, but perhaps it at least will get us to a first approximation to the truth. For the Sufi, the inner quest is seen in relation to Allah, who is the supreme object of worship and of Islamic ritual. It is true that some Sufis (dangerously from the point of view of the traditionalists) re-described God in ways which are reminiscent of Advaita Vedanta. But orthodoxy succeeded in maintaining an interpretative context in which God remains the Other and mysticism is still seen in the context of worship. Similar remarks can be made about medieval and late medieval Christian mysticism. But very differently, Theravada Buddhism, though not denying the gods, never saw the mystical quest in the context of worship, nor was nirvana in any way identified with the supreme object of worship. Mahayana of course came to project *bhakti* and celestial Buddhas, but leaving aside the Pure Land and one or two other movements, the contemplative goal of suchness, the Void, was considered to be the heart of the quest and transcending the Buddha as object of worship (for his true nature, the *Dharmakaya*, is the Void). In Advaita Vedanta likewise that Brahman-Atman which the liberated individual realises transcends the personal Lord or Īśvara who is worshipped in ordinary religion. Briefly then and crudely, in some religious traditions, mysticism is seen firmly in the context of worship; in others, worship is subordinated to the mystical path; in others, worship is more or less irrelevant to the mystical quest. Still in most religions God or the gods are significant, and so likewise is the contemplative life. It is natural for worship and contemplation to fuse together in some way.

I now turn to make some remarks on the moving submission by Brother David Steindl-Rast. Much of what he says about listening is highly reminiscent of Brother Lawrence's beautiful *The Practice of the Presence of God*; but I take it that though part of what he says is contemplative in character (e.g. about the tangerine -- regarding which a Buddhist would say like things, save only about its being 'pure gift': here the emphasis would be rather different) part also is a description of Christian obedience which need not be especially mystical in character. Again we are confronted, I think, by the two faces of religion, *bhakti*, i.e. devotion to God, and the path of inner contemplation. It is for this reason, I suspect, that Brother David wishes to moderate the duality implicit in worship; and his suggestions about how to interpret the Trinity are highly significant.

Yet still we notice a rich context of Christian living -- the Bible, the Benedictine rule, the use of the Jesus Prayer. How essential are these traditions? It might be answered: each tradition is a discipline and a context; and such disciplines and contexts are rafts to liberation. And here we meet with the problem: Is it then in the last resort indifferent which raft I sail on? In that case, any public truth as we understand it would seem to disappear, and religious doctrine itself becomes instrumental rather than authoritative. Yet this seems an unstable position, for without belief in the truth of (for instance) the word of the Bible how does Brother David derive his discipline of 'listening'? We can see the attractions of the Perennial Philosophy and of neo-Vedanta as expounded by Swami Prabuddhananda and his colleagues: for this contains a theory of truth combined with a theory of the relativism of aspects at least of the various religious traditions. However, that neo-Vedanta itself in the process becomes an alternative doctrinal scheme to the others, and so itself enters the arena of both interreligious dialogue and rivalry. For it is by no means obvious that mystical motifs by themselves should or could be determinative of truth in religion. In brief, other considerations may also be vital -- prophetic vision, moral insight, historical relevance, consistency, fruitfulness and so on.

I referred earlier to the need not to be too disheartened by the problems of comparison of the experience of mystics in diverse traditions and even within one tradition. There is fortunately a growing body of useful and sensitive literature in this front (well surveyed) by Peter Moore in *Religion*, vol. 3, p. 146ff. But there are still large, indeed immense, gaps in our knowledge; yet the time is a ripe one for a more systematic and intense exploration of the field. Though I have reservations about some aspects of his argument, I would consider that one important approach is through the methods advocated by J.F. Staal in his recent *Exploring Mysticism* (University of California Press, and Penguin Books, 1976). But a great deal of literary work remains to be done, and such recent pioneering works as R.C. Zaehner's *Mysticism Sacred and Profane* suffered from lack of an application of the phenomenological method. This perhaps is where analytic philosophy can be useful in trying to clarify ways of distinguishing between relatively ramified and relatively unramified descriptions of inner experience, i.e. between those descriptions which contain much interpretative loading and others which contain relatively little. Thus we can approach comparison at two levels -- one through the comparative study of doctrines and myths (the source of interpretative loading) and another through attempting a phenomenology of types of mystical experience. I feel that very much more needs to be done on this front, and that the results could be valuable practically and would illuminate the philosophical question of the relations between types of religious experience and religious truth claims.

Unity and Diversity in the Interpretation of Mysticism
By TERENCE PENELHUM

I.

The philosopher is never where the action is. He is always someone who tries to interpret and evaluate the activities and experiences of others. This conference gives us, as philosophers, an
unusual opportunity of being closer to the action than usual.

Two opposite things strike a philosopher about what our practitioners have said. The first is a remarkable similarity in what
they say about their experience and techniques. The second is
the presence, throughout, of apparently radical differences.
Philosophical discussions of mysticism have tended to concentrate
around two questions. First, how real are the differences, and
can they be interpreted in a manner which allows us to talk of
mystical experience as a distinct and fundamentally single form
of consciousness? Second, if we can talk of it in this way, is
it, in philosophical jargon, cognitive, or noetic, rather than
delusory? Professor Hick has offered us a framework within which
the differences between the mystics (and indeed between all the
various forms of religious experience) are culturally-relative
signs of a higher, noumenal, reality which impinges on men's consciousness if they permit it to do so. Professor Smart seems
more perturbed by the doctrinal diversity among mystics, and
stresses the extent to which the practice of contemplation itself
goes forward by the use of devotional acts that are saturated by
different doctrinal commitments. I have no settled view on these
matters, but want instead to air some philosophical anxieties that
beset me whenever I reflect on these two questions.

II.

Let me begin by mentioning some of the likenesses that I think we
all find in the accounts before us. Each practitioner speaks of
the highest experience vouchsafed to him in the language of union.
Each speaks of it as something which is vouchsafed -- the passive
voice seems necessary when speaking of it. Yet it comes only
after dedicated spiritual activity, which involves moral discipline, the negation of distraction and spiritual clutter, and the
invocation and assertion of the presence of the transcendent in
the self. These, broadly, are the likenesses; and they are the
likenesses which have always served to distinguish mystical experience from religious experience of other kinds. Insofar as these
other kinds are included in what our mystics speak of to us, they
appear as preparatory to the unitive experience. They may indeed

be part of the mystic way, but it is not their presence that
makes the mystic way *mystical*. The differences are all differences in what Professor Smart has called doctrinal presuppositions. Each speaks to us of his experience and practice in the
language of a particular religious tradition, which embodies doctrines about the relation of man to the transcendent. These doctrines have some likenesses (Rabbi Schachter is particularly concerned to draw attention to these, in order to contest W.T.
Stace's claim that Jewish mysticism is not mystical) but analogy
is far from identity in doctrinal matters.

Now there is an implied assumption in the way in which both Professor Hick and Professor Smart approach this combination of likeness and difference. It is one which philosophers generally make
when they talk about the second of my two questions. The assumption is this: that the presence of doctrinal diversity in the language the mystics use, to themselves and to us, represents a barrier to a positive estimate of their experience and practice.
Professor Smart tells us not to be disheartened by it; Professor
Hick classifies the differences as merely phenomenal. Both seem
to say that if we accept that there is a distinctive mystical form
of consciousness, we can only be confident that it is not delusory
through and through if we can reconcile the differences between
what one mystic says and what another says. I think this is a
most unrealistic assumption. I want to put a question-mark
against it, and to suggest that it, too, is culturally conditioned.

Let me make a couple of simple comparisons. The first comparison is this. Moral thinkers have been struck by the fact that
men in many times and places manifest a sense of duty or obligation: that they feel themselves bound in one way or another to
put aside their personal wishes and follow their consciences.
Some thinkers have gone on to say that this widespread phenomenon
shows men to have a special moral sense that alerts them to their
duties; and they have given it an honoured place in their analyses
of human nature. Others, however, have been struck by the fact
that what men's consciences tell them to do varies enormously from
place to place -- think only of our attitudes to practices like
infanticide and senicide; and they have gone on to say that the
moral sense is wholly delusory, that the wise man will not accept
it as his guide to action at any time. Now one can defend moral-
ity against this form of scepticism by underplaying the differences between different moral codes, or by saying that it is not
morally important what you think your duty is, provided you do
whatever you think to be your duty. But one does not have to proceed this way, because there is another possibility. Perhaps
there is indeed a specifically moral form of consciousness, and it
is potentially a source of truth, but not a guaranteed source of

truth. Perhaps it can sometimes go wrong. Perhaps the other forms of belief and attitude that coexist with it must be the right ones before conscience itself can be a reliable guide to moral choice.

My second comparison is this. Plato, Aristotle, Spinoza, and Leibniz all created metaphysical systems which evaluate man's place in the universe, place scientific knowledge in a wider context, and support moral conclusions. Each system can provide the person who has done the intellectual and imaginative labour necessary to understand it with a profound vision that he could not get otherwise. All these systems are distinguishable in these respects from the undeveloped and unsystematic reflections of common-sense, and from the sceptical and anti-metaphysical philosophies of (say) a Hume or a Wittgenstein. It would not naturally occur to us to say, as a result of these similarities, that the doctrinal differences between them are merely superficial differences that mask a deeper identity of intent. For the similarities are the similarities that exist between those who accept a certain manner of proceeding in philosophy but get different results from it. If Spinoza is right, then what Leibniz says is false. Profound, yes, but you can be profound and wrong. If you say that the differences between Spinoza and Leibniz are in some way not real differences, this is a way of rejecting both, not of accepting either.

Suppose we now agree that there is a distinct mystical mode of consciousness that is integrated with other forms of religious experience but is not identical with any of them. Suppose we also agree that these connections result in substantial doctrinal differences. I agree that these differences do not show that mystical consciousness is delusory. But in order to reject this negative conclusion we do not have to say that all mystical experience is experience of a reality to which the varying doctrinal responses are somehow ultimately equivalent. We *can* say this, but there is another possibility: that this mode of consciousness can sometimes lead to real union and sometimes only to the semblance of it. Perhaps doctrine is not an obfuscatory set of pointers to a higher reality that cannot be doctrinally understood, but mystical experience is a reward which is only noetic when sought and found in the context of the right set of doctrines.

If we reject this possibility *a priori*, why do we? I would like to suggest that we must at least be on our guard against a form of cultural conditioning of our own that makes us too readily angry with doctrinal differences, and makes us a little too ecumenical for our own good. In our day and age we are apt to be struck primarily by the difference there is between those who are willing to participate in the mystical (or for that matter, any other) form of religious consciousness, and those who reject it altogether.

73

So keen are we to assert the importance of openness to the mystical way that we are quite unwilling to accept the theoretical possibility that one can follow it and go wrong; and the only way of not conceding this is to deny the ultimate importance of the different directions followed by those whose forms of experience are psychologically similar to one another. Negatively, this often takes the form of equating secularity with frivolity and closed-mindedness. Positively, it often takes the form of equating the religious consciousness with seriousness and openness. While such connections do, in my view, exist, they are not universal. But the temptation to make the equations is a natural response to an era in which adherents of all religious traditions are faced with the spread of secularity, and want to believe that the doctrinal differences that separate them can be put aside to enable them to face a common enemy. I think that this is an invasion of religion by the criteria of secular politics, but I will not try to argue this. The moral I do want to draw is this: let us not assume the differences between our respondents are necessarily less fundamental than their similarities, or that a philosophical interpretation of what they have said must presuppose a unitary significance. Let us proceed in hope; and let us, as philosophers, take with deep seriousness the recognition which the practising mystics show for one another. But let us not assume that reality must accord with our spiritual preferences. Or that he who feels he has to reject, however respectfully, what a fellow-seeker has to say is, for that reason, not listening.

III.

I would now like to make a second, related point about the significance of the differences between mystical experiences as they are found in varied religious traditions. The problem of unity and diversity does not just arise in relation to the significance of what the mystic says, but arises equally in connection with the significance of ritual and worship, prophecy and vision. It is therefore quite natural to find Professor Hick electing to treat the question of the cognitive character of mystical experience in the wider context of religious experience in general. He appears to prefer a very wide understanding of the word "mysticism" which includes not only unitive experience but also all first-hand religion. Professor Smart concerns himself particularly with the interrelationship between contemplative techniques and worship, confining the word "mystical" to the former. There is no harm in this semantic difference when the context tells us which use is intended. I myself shall use the word "mystical" and its cognates

in the more restricted way. But the difference can serve to
draw our attention to a very important fact about the relationship between the special questions concerning the nature and
status of mystical experience in the special sense, and the
general questions to which Professor Hick has addressed himself
about the nature and status of all forms of religious experience.
The fact is this: the major religious traditions of the world
do not merely differ in the doctrinal interpretations they offer
of religious experience. They also differ markedly in the
relative importance or centrality accorded to one sort of
religious experience as opposed to another.

Mystical experience issues, as we have seen, in utterances of
a special kind, that say that the one vouchsafed it is one with,
is a moment of, is not set in duality over against, the Transcendent. This language demarcates *mystical* experience from
religious experience of other kinds. But it does not come to
us "neat". It comes mixed with speech that emanates from a tradition that also incorporates other practices and experiences.
And each tradition places a different value on one kind of experience and practice relative to another. There is a very great
difference between thinking of worship and devotional practice
as primarily a mode of disciplining and liberating the soul for
the ultimate reception of the unitive experience, and thinking of
the latter experience as one available to a minority as a special
divine dispensation to a soul that has already attained spiritual
resolution in some other mode of religious life. Associated with
this difference there will be a difference in the centrality accorded the great mystical figures in the determination of the
character of the religious traditions to which they belong, and a
difference in the importance attached to the precise nature of the
pronouncements they make. While I am subject to authoritative
contradiction in a gathering such as this, it can hardly be doubt-
ed that the importance accorded the mystic in the Hindu and Buddhist traditions is vastly greater than that accorded the mystic
in any of the three major Western traditions; that in the three
Western traditions the mystic does not determine, but merely
enriches, the tradition; that what he says deepens, but does not
fundamentally redirect, the religious experience sought after
as a norm by others in the tradition; and that in so far as his
experience requires him to bend and twist the language that
the tradition provides him to talk of it, what he then says
will be something that the tradition will not try to direct
itself by, but merely to *accommodate* -- and in the end may
accommodate, if it must, by treating as an anomaly. On the
other hand, a tradition like that represented by Swami
Prabuddhananda, which regards the mystic as the normative spirit-

ual figure, will interpret doctrinal differences as of little consequence if they express diverse ways of preparing men to follow
in his footsteps.

I would infer two things. First, that even if we find the most
striking similarities between mystics of different traditions, we
cannot happily deduce that this shows a corresponding unity of
significance or ultimate meaning between the *traditions*, for
these traditions vary in how much the mystic represents them.
Second, even though Professor Hick may be wise in raising questions about the significance of religious experience in general,
rather than mystical experience *per se*, we are more likely to
follow him in stressing the unity against the diversity if we sit
among a group of mystics than if we compare religious traditions
in their totality.

IV.

Having made all these remarks in order to emphasise the diversity we find among mystics, and its potential importance for the
philosopher of religion, I want to turn to the unity we also find.
I want to suggest that the very unity that we find among the mystics is itself a barrier to a particular way of coming to terms
with the diversity! I am sorry to spin conceits: let me explain
what I mean.

Professor Hick has introduced here a notion which he has put to
very penetrating use elsewhere in the analysis of religious experience -- the notion of "experiencing-as". I do not need to repeat his explanation, but it is a development, as he says, of
some remarks of Wittgenstein. Wittgenstein comments on the fact
that an ambiguous picture can be "seen as" quite different things
by different people -- and also can be "seen as" different things
by one and the same person at different times. Hick widens the
notion from "seeing-as" to "experiencing-as", in order to incor-
porate within it our power to interpret all aspects of our common
experience in different ways. The application of the notion of
experiencing-as requires the postulation of three elements: a
common or shared *object* to be interpreted (to correspond to the
picture that is to be seen one way or another), two or more individual *subjects* to do the interpreting, and finally, of course,
two or more resultant interpretations *by* the subjects *of* the object. I do not think it would be a fair criticism of this model
to say that it requires that there be some neutral description of
the common object which both subjects could accept before moving
to their alternative interpretations -- even though there would be
such a common description in the case of ambiguous pictures. But
it does seem to follow from this model that the object can be in

some manner *identified* in common by those who understand it in different ways: though this would be a very sticky requirement to spell out.

The experiencing-as model is very helpful in expressing the difference between the mode of experience of the religious believer and that of the secular man or woman. Here the common object is our common perceptible environment, with all its goods and evils; and each interprets it in differing ways, while continuing to co-exist with the other within it. The model also leaves it open to say, as Hick does, that each of us can exercise some degree of *choice* whether to interpret this common world in a secular or a religious fashion. The model also has a natural use in representing the differences between alternative religious traditions. Here one can go in two directions. One can either take the common object to be, once again, our common world or some part of it, in which case (say) the Christian and Islamic worldviews would be two interpretations, and the secular world-view a third one alongside them; or one can say instead that the common object is one whose existence or reality is only recognised by religious believers and is not even open for interpretation by the secular man. Each way has difficulties, because each seems to jeopardise the neutrality of the model. To say that the object is once again the common world or some part of it seems to concede too much to the secularist, who is insisting all along that there is no possible object beyond the common world; but to say that the object is something beyond the common world concedes him too little. Professor Hick actually uses his experiencing-as model in both ways. He uses it in the first way when he takes as the common object religious *experience*. This is something which the unbeliever will regard as delusory, but he will agree that it exists in our common world, so he and the believer can disagree about how to interpret it, while agreeing on what is is that they are differently interpreting. Hick argues persuasively for the view that a positive interpretation of it is at least rational. I hasten past the difficult question: can an unbeliever interpret religious experience negatively while at the same time himself *having* it? or is it a necessary truth that anyone who has it will interpret it in some positive manner? But while I hasten past this, I must linger a little on an allied question.

This question is the following. If one takes the common object that is differently interpreted to be some kind of *experience*, this seems to imply too neat a distinction between an experience and the interpretation of it. Is this really possible for anyone other than a person who regards it as an illusion? To explain: the secularist will reject mystical experience, while agreeing that it happens *to others*. So for him the experience and the interpretation are obviously distinct. But what about the two mystics who speak of their experience in doctrinally opposite

77

ways, e.g. in personal or impersonal language? Can we glibly say that they are offering different interpretations of *one and the same experience*? Do we have a common object of interpretation at all? How do we tell? What is to correspond to the independently identifiable ambiguous picture? When someone tells me that two friends have been presented with the same ambiguous picture and one has seen it as a duck and the other as a rabbit, I want to say that although they have been looking at the same object, they have had different experiences. But in our present case we have to locate one and the same experience in order to have a common object. Most of us, reading and listening to our practising mystics, will feel somewhat torn, but will indeed want to say that they share experiences which they are interpreting differently. Here I think Professor Smart's distinction between ramified and unramified descriptions is important. If we wanted to prove to someone that the mystics had the same experience we would have to produce, from their statements, a number of closely similar unramified descriptions -- descriptions that did not contain much language that entailed one doctrinal scheme and excluded another. If we were able to do this, then we could reasonably say that each was having the same (i.e. a phenomenologically similar) experience that the other was having, and interpreting it in different ways. This would leave it open, of course, for the sceptic to say that this shared experience was interpreted mistakenly by all of them, and offer his own negative reading of it.

While reasonable, this application of the idea of experiencing-as does leave some philosophical difficulties behind it. In the first place, it is always somewhat arbitrary to decide when an experience ends and an interpretation begins, and it is in consequence always open to someone to insist that the line cannot be drawn anywhere. More important, however, is this: there is, in one obvious sense, no such thing as one common experience, in the sense of one numerically identical experience shared by several people. There are at best several numerically distinct but exactly similar experiences. The single common object in the case of the ambiguous picture is the picture -- something drawn on paper or projected on a screen. Philosophers present will no doubt recall all the difficulties that arise in the philosophy of perception if one tries to say that there is also some mental element that is common to all the percipients who see the picture, in addition to their differing perceptions of it as a duck or a rabbit. Even though they can give a neutral common description of the picture, this does not yield a common mental object, but an agreed abstraction from a diverse set of differing interpretations, which is not the same thing.

Yet all these difficulties are merely that -- difficulties. I myself think that they do not prevent one from using the experiencing-as model to talk of mystical experience as containing a common core of phenomenologically similar elements that are fairly described as one and the same experience variously interpreted. On the whole, however, this is not the way in which Professor Hick chooses to use his experiencing-as model of analysis. He does not, for most of his paper, talk of the common object as the mystics' shared *experience*. Instead he talks of the common object as the Transcendent. This immediately excludes the secular interpretation as an interpretation of a common object, since the secularist cannot admit that religious experience, *defined as experience of the Transcendent*, ever occurs. I can only speculate on Hick's reasons for choosing to talk in this way, but two possible ones occur to me. The first is that he might feel that if he did not talk in this way -- in a way, that is, which presupposes in identifying the common object which all mystics experience that there is indeed a Transcendent reality -- he would yield a point to the sceptic. The sceptic might say that the very variety of mystical interpretations was itself an argument against accepting the truth of any of them. If one defines the experience as experience of the Transcendent then of course one blocks that contention. The second reason he might have is one I have already expressed anxiety about: he might feel that by identifying the common object of interpretation as the Transcendent he will also weaken the suggestion that one form of mystical experience is more nearly veridical than another. I do not myself feel persuaded by either consideration, if either did in fact move him. The fact that the sceptic cannot admit the existence of that which you define as the common object of religious experience is not a philosophical advantage, but the contrary, and the fact that your identification of the common object entails that all the diverse interpretations are partially right seems to me to be an advantage only from the point of view of considerations other than that of truth.

But let us leave all this, and consider the suggestions that Professor Hick does make. He says that different forms of religious experience are different ways of experiencing the Transcendent, or Infinite Spirit. To accommodate the most radical of these differences, such as the interpretation of it as personal and impersonal, he invokes the Kantian distinction between noumenon and phenomenon -- the distinction between that which is independent of human consciousness and yet appears to it, and the interpreted appearance that it presents to a particular consciousness. He amends Kant in more than one way, the primary way being the claim that the forms of *phenomena* are not universal, but culturally conditioned. The ultimate object of religious experience is beyond human description, but is experienced as the varyingly described Absolutes of the different religious traditions. It can be shut out of the consciousness of a person (or a culture) altogether; but if it is admitted, if it is allowed to appear to human consciousness, it does so in the manner determined by the traditional influences that have helped to mould that particular consciousness.

Attractive and valuable though this is in other contexts, I think that *mystical* experience does not admit this sort of under-standing. My reason is that the unity of which the mystics speak calls into question the whole framework within which it is here being understood. The difference between other forms of religious experience and the claims of the mystics seems to me to matter critically here. For worship and devotional experience do indeed seem to occur in a manner which necessarily preserves the distinct-ness and otherness of men and the divine, and here it is wholly intelligible to say that the way the Other divine is perceived is a result of the particular situation of the human consciousness that perceives it and worships it. But does one not claim to be beyond this if one claims to experience mystic union? To use Kantian language a little more: a phenomenon is, according to Kant, necessarily that which appears to a human conscious subject. Without a conscious individual subject, or a multiplicity of them, there would be no phenomena. There would, of course, "be" noumena. But the distinction between the noumenon, and that to which it appears so that it is experienced as a phenomenon, is essential. (In Kantian language, the self is noumenal also.) It is this very distinction which is characteristically denied in those accounts of mystical experience in which the diverse mystics most regularly agree. My point is simply that distinctively mys-tical experience is the one sort of religious experience where the duality of subject and noumenon seems not to be applicable. Mys-tical experience may indeed be experience of the Transcendent, but not (necessarily not) *as phenomenon*. The use of the Kantian framework may be wholly correct in helping us cope with the vari-ety of perceptions of the Transcendent with which men's religious life abounds. But it cannot subsume within it the distinctive experience of the mystic. For the mystic does not seem to be "experiencing-as" at all.

V.

If these comments on Professor Hick's argument are sound ones, it seems to me that we are left with the problem of diversity in a very intractable form. Let me restate it. It does seem that there is a common core of experience and interpretation that is distinctively mystical; but that it is always found in those who experience it interlocked with doctrinal commitments that vary to

the point of apparent incompatibility between one person and another, and which affect the perception of the personal disciplines
that mystical experience requires. Unless we are willing to dismiss all mystical experience as delusory, the unity we find makes
us look for some way of reducing the doctrinal differences, of
making the discord concordant, as Zaehner might say. As far as I
can see, there are only two ways, and one has to choose between
them.

(1) The first way is to work from within a doctrinal framework,
interpret the mystics' experiences in the language of that doctrinal framework, and say that the experience of mystics in *other*
traditions, though it parallels the experience of mystics in the
one within which you work, is nevertheless incomplete, misleading,
or non-cognitive to the very extent to which it is interpreted in
ways inconsistent with the doctrines you hold. This way forces us
into different judgments upon similar experiences in the light of
their doctrinal contexts, and consequently presupposes in an obvious way the primacy of doctrine over mystical experience.

(2) The alternative way is to insist that the common features of
the mystics' experiences must override the differences between
the doctrines that interlock with them in the traditions where
they are found; and that the various incompatible doctrines are
all expressions of the varying ways men have experienced the
Transcendent reality which is known and shared directly in the
mystic's experience. This way requires us to subordinate all doctrinal requirements to the recognition of the common features of
the mystics' experience, in a very strong manner: we have to say
that the mystic, in so far as he does not himself indulge in doctrinal pronouncements of the kind which divide the traditions,
has transcended the limitations which the differences between the
doctrines reveal. *His* experience is not phenomenal, but literally
unitive in the way he is impelled to say it is.

Which way one chooses will depend on many factors. One of
these, no doubt, will be the presence or absence of mystical experience in one's own life. Another will be the relation one has to
a particular religious tradition, and whether it is itself one
which gives a central or peripheral place to mystical experience.
But whatever the causes, no philosopher can invent any *grounds*
for decision that do not beg all the questions.

Comments on Penelhum*
By JOHN HICK

I would like to say something about the comments which Professor
Penelhum made about the "experiencing-as" approach, for which I
am very grateful indeed. Curiously enough, I do not think we
differ very much; I may turn out to be over-ecumenical again,
but I do not think so.

I will go back to the earlier part of his paper for a moment.
He wants to keep open the possibility that all forms of religious
experience, except, presumably, one might be delusory. The experiencing-as analysis does permit this. It does not either
commend it or discommend it, but leaves it as an open possibility
to be decided on other grounds. I do not want to say that the
mystics have the same experience and then interpret it differently, because if anyone said that they would mean by "interpret",
I think, "form theories about". In the sense in which I wish to
use the word, interpretation enters into the experience, so that
they have different experiences in which different concepts
are at work, and then, of course, on the basis of their different
experiences they develop different theologies. But the hypothesis was that in these different experiences (and I want to
say that they are very different indeed) we have different
phenomenal appearances of the same divine noumenon. This is not
to say that these varying divine phenomena all relate us to the
noumenon equally adequately, because the divine phenomenon is a
joint product of the divine noumenon and a human contribution.
The human contribution is a set of human concepts and categories,
and these concepts and categories may be more adequate in some
cases than in others. If religion is a way of being aware of as
much of the transcendent as we are prepared to put up with at the
moment, or as much of the transcendent as we are prepared to
respond to with our whole lives, or as much as the tradition in
which we are allows us to respond to, then naturally there
might be many differences between traditions, including the
difference that some may enable you to respond more to the
transcendent than others. As far as this analysis is concerned,
we are not committed on whether all the divine phenomena are,
as it were, on the same level in relation to the divine noumenon
or not. If one wanted to go on to discuss whether they are or
not this would be a different discussion.

Professor Penelhum has made the very important point that you
cannot apply the "experiencing-as" analysis, in which there is
an experiencer and something that he experiences-as such-and-
such, to a unitary situation, because if there is unity there is
no subject and no object. I think this is right, but on the

other hand a very qualified truth, or rather a truth with a very
qualified application. Let us remember that if we mean by
"mysticism" the actual experience of unity with the transcendent,
I do not think any of our practising mystics here have said
that they have had this ultimate experience of total and absolute
unity with ultimate reality. (I may be wrong, and would like to
have this confirmed or otherwise.) I do not think I have ever
met anyone who has said that they have had that experience.
Whenever anyone has something somewhat approaching it, the mere
fact that they can come back and tell us means that they have
retained their individuality and the individual memory of the
experience. This suggests to me that this is not the ultimate
experience which our different traditions postulate. So the
difficulty of restricting the use of the word "mysticism"
to this unitive experience is that then there is no mysticism:
it is a heavenly reality but not an earthly reality. On the
other hand, if by "mysticism" we mean the various degrees of
religious experience right up to that, then this is a reality
but is susceptible of subject-object, experiencing-as analysis.
So I think we have to accept Professor Penelhum's point, but I
must point out that there may be no one around to whose experience it applies: not only no one around locally, but no one in
the whole world.

*Transcript of spoken remarks.

The Buddhist Path
By HERBERT V. GUENTHER

In presenting Buddhism in the Western Language, I feel a certain
uneasiness in view of the fact that there is an inherent problem
in fitting Buddhism into a conceptual scheme to which our Western interpreters are so accustomed. However, because the
medium of our communicative language is English and because the
use of Sanskrit terms aids only to "mystify" instead of clarify-
ing the issue, I wish to keep Sanskrit and other Buddhist technical terms to a minimum.

Whenever we talk about Buddhism, we must be careful not to
obscure the information in the texts, but must present the material in view of what the Buddhist texts themselves have to say,
and the texts inform us that Buddhism declares itself to be a
path.

The word "path" or "way" is usually interpreted as that which
leads one from one place to another; thus, scholars have understood the Buddhist path as a path which leads one from *saṁsāra*
to *nirvāna*. However, as *saṁsāra* is none other than *nirvāna* and
nirvāna is no place else but where there is *saṁsāra*, a path
cannot lead from point "a" to point "b". So where is the path
to lead? By the term "path" the Buddhist implied the unity of
feelings and cognitions wherein the term "path" is a compre-
hensive term for what in abstract language we call goal-conscious-
ness and goal-directed striving and development. Therefore, when
Buddhism declares that it is a path leading to a goal that is
realizable by man, it always insists on knowledge born of the
desire to cultivate and refine the personality and of the need
to find deliverance, both of which go together and are deeply
felt as they develop and grow in the individual.

Man's being-in-the-world, which is more precisely his being-
his-world, is a system in the specific sense of a system-from-
within which is the integral unity of that about which a thinking person thinks; however, the problem of man's being is pecul-
iarly difficult because man is not just an object among other
objects -- just like anything else. Rather, in experiencing
himself as an object, he is intended as being reflexively related
to himself as subject in a double manner: sense-perceptively and
in action. This means that in learning more about a situation,
man learns more about himself. This learning begins with a
"response" to a situation -- a tension field -- which solicits
a response and which is itself the response. In describing this
dynamic process, we talk about the "subject" and "object", but
since the person is his own situation -- the solicitation of a

response and the response itself -- the subject-object division
cannot be maintained. There is evidence for this. I cannot
help but speak to you as a "subject" and you are the "object"
of my addressing you. But vice-versa, I am the "object" of your
observation. What am I? Subject? Object? Every person alive
refuses to be treated merely as an object simply because he feels
himself to be "subject". But as I have just pointed out, the
"subject" in view of my observation is "object" and the "object"
in view of its observation is "subject". Therefore, the Buddhists have pointed out that the subject-object dichotomy, although real in a general and operation sense (*saṁvṛti- satya*,
is like a misinterpretation of what is primary (*paramārtha-satya*).
In this sense, *anātman* does not mean "no-self" or "no ego", but
points to the rule that we cannot have an abiding principle which
we call an ego or a self and that when one hypothesizes these as
primary, one has done sloppy reasoning. In view of the path,
therefore, the human situation is a tension-field, which is in
constant activity and in constant play wherein any response in it
changes also the whole situation, and this progress or process has
been termed the *Path of Learning (saṁbhāra-mārga)* or the *Path of
Preparation* which traditionally has meant the accumulation of
knowledge and merits.

The word "knowledge" (*prajñā*) has a special significance in
Buddhism in that it is primary and the Tibetans have translated
it *Ye-shes* -- that knowing which has been there since every
beginning -- thus showing that they understood this very significance. In the Western tradition, whenever a "beginning" is talked about, it is understood as a historical beginning; however,
the Buddhists were quite clear that when they talked about a
beginning, they were talking about it in a logical sense. In
other words, the Buddhists realized that one must make a start
somewhere and that "somewhere" was not a historically significant somewhere, but a logically significant one. For example,
this particular session of the Mysticism Conference began at
3:30 P.M., but were that point a historically significant beginning, we could ask of it "What was before that?" But since it is,
after all, a logical beginning, we accept the fact that previously there was something and on the basis of that acceptance, we
begin our discussion. So it is in this sense that the Buddhists
talk about a beginning and the beginning on the path begins
with the fundamental question, "What does it mean to be?" This
question implies a dialectical process. That is, the more I
learn about a situation, the better I can deal with it and the
better I can deal with a situation, the more I can learn about
it. Therefore, the path can be understood in terms of growth or
development which is the expansion or the widening of knowledge,
because the situation contains, as it were, the knowledge.
Knowledge, therefore, is not brought to a situation from the

outside, but is there, so to speak, in the very individual who is
his world and who is, as an embodying being, constantly embodying psychic life. We do not infer, to give an example, that if
somebody blushes he is ashamed, but the blushing *is* his shame.
Thus, knowledge is that capacity that each of us has to distinguish and to appreciate between what is helpful, what is further-
ing, and what is value, because in ordinary life, it is not with
things which we deal, but with meanings and values. That I study
a subject is an indication that the subject has value for me and
that it also means something to me. It need not have a pre-
determined meaning, which may turn out to be meaningless after all!

The texts define knowledge (*prajñā*) as the analysis, the separation of the *dharma*. In the English language, we talk about *the
dharma*, but the *Vyākhyā Yukti*, attributed to Vasubandhu, gives
ten different indications for the usage of this term. Thus, in
understanding the significance of this first phase of the path,
we must take into consideration what the Buddhists meant by the
word *dharma*. Thus, *dharma* (ie. that which is to be analysized)
in the context of this first phase of the path is "man's being-
in-the-world, which more precisely is his being-his-world."
This observation indicates that man is part of the constant on-
going embodiment in which his very bodily presence is constantly changing the whole constituent of the situation. The body is
not only the most precious possession that one has, but it is
also the focal point of one's orientation. But man is not
merely a physical entity; he has feelings and the capacity for
thought. For example, one feels that a particular situation is
unpleasant, unpleasant because of the tension which demands a
solution. This means that one must inspect the situation and this
process of inspection is definitely a mental process. During
this activity, many logical constructions occur and of those one
is man's search for stability in this ever changing picture. The
process of logical constructs which go into making up our world
is an on-going process, but this does not imply that, as a consequence, the world must be a "mental construct." In other
words, the view of the world which we hold may in fact be a
mental construct, but this does not necessitate that the world be
one.

Thus, the statement, "man being-his-world" implies an on-
going process which assumes new use and new meanings which are not
simply received from the situation but which are also brought to
it. This means, the situation is simply there and the "there-
ness" (*pratibhāsa*) is primary. What we do with it is secondary.
It is the secondary aspect which, however, has fascinated us to
the degreee that we have been drawn more and more into it, to
the point that we firmly believe that the "logical constructs"
are the final word. But they break and disappoint. Thus, those

"logical constructs," because of their very nature to break and disappoint, are the beginning point on the Buddhist Path. If we should proceed from this beginning, which is a dialectical process between learning and enacting, and hence, a process of growth, then this task takes us to the next stage.

Indians on the whole, and Buddhists in particular, have been keen observers. Theirs is the claim: "Let us first observe before we theorize!" Their observation led to the second path, the *Path of Linking-up (prayoga-marga)*, which comprises four levels of progression.

The first of those is called "warmth." We express this phase when, in our own language, we use such expressions as "warming up to a subject." In this phase, the distinction between "body" and "mind" cannot be made, because this "warmth" is both a mental warming up and a physical one. Thus in dealing with this first level, we find that our normal categories of "body" and "mind" do not apply.

As one warms up to a subject and becomes more and more involved, he reaches a certain intensity in his pursuit. This intensity is the second level.

Both "warmth" and "intensity" are pathways on which we can proceed as well as fall back. Their main function is to lead us to a more vivid realization and a deeper understanding of the nature of the constituents of our reality.

When through three stages, intensity has reached its peak, there occurs an event which is of greatest importance but of momentary duration. It is an acceptance, the third level, of the validity of the truths which one has experienced. This third level also has three stages. Out of the third stage results what is known as the "highest worldly realization," which is the fourth level. Acceptance and the highest worldly realization are the culminating points of the modifiable process. The highest worldly realization gives one the first glance of what may constitute a possible solution to the tension situation which one has been trying to analyze, to understand, or to put into perspective. It is this fourth level which acts as the impetus to carry one through to the next stage and which due to its very function constitutes the *Path of Seeing (darśāna-marga)*.

Seeing (*darśāna*) is the impetus which carries one through to the next stage, because when one has stopped looking and senses a feeling of satisfaction with what has been seen, then one has come to the end of one's quest and that is *siddhānta*, a static view of reality. The distinction between *darśāna* (having a good look) and *siddhānta* (a sense of satisfaction with what has been attained) lies in the fact that, of the *siddhānta*, one can always press one into having another look. Thus, on the Buddhist Path, the confrontation with a situation -- the first glance at what may constitute a possible solution -- is also the third path, the

Path of Seeing. It is here that the first Noble Truth (*duḥkha-satya* - the reality of frustrations) is truly seen and wherein the Buddha subsequently proclaimed the Four Noble Truths. In other words, it was in this moment of the highest worldly real-ization which was the glimpse into the possible solution for a tension situation and which resulted from having accepted the situation which vibrates with a tremendous impetus to push on-ward , that the Buddha realized a new perspective of a situation which has always been there. It was not that he saw something which was not there previously, but he could now put what he saw into a new perspective.

This new perspective is an experience that surpasses every-thing that went before it. Its emotional quality, which is one of pure joy, is derived from this glimpse of reality-as-it-is. It is receptive in the sense that it can "let be" not only in the moment of seeing, but also subsequently. This joy is known as the first "spiritual level" (*bhūmi*). This joy is momentary and therefore it is from the second "spiritual level", that of the Stainless One, that one begins to deal with what one has seen. It is the act of bringing to life a force which counteracts negative trends which have always dragged one into unpleasant situations.

The act of bringing this force to life is the fourth path, the *Path of Cultivation (bhāvanā-marga)*. *Bhāvanā* has been translated variously and the one most familiar to us is probably "contem-plation." Literally, *bhāvanā* means: "to bring to life." It derives from the causative form of the Sanskrit verb-root *bhū* which means: "to be"; "to exist." The process of "bringing to life" may involve a number of various techniques which, in the Buddhist context, refer to the other so-called "spiritual levels." Depending upon the Buddhist text from which one derives his in-formation, these "spiritual levels" vary in number. Again, the most familiar to us is probably the number ten which derives from the *Daśabhūmika Sūtra*. In any event, the process of "bringing to life" continues as one traverses through the various "spiri-tual levels" which aid one in dismantling the fortress of the ego-construct. As I have pointed out earlier, the "ego" is nothing more than a logical construct in view of the fact that any attempt to reduce an on-going process to some abiding principle is a sign of sloppy reasoning and the resulting logical construct of the ego functions as a defence mechanism which by its very strength calls forth what are known as "emotions" into play. The *Path of Cultivation* is, therefore, the phase in which something is done about the "conceptualizing process" which impoverishes one's view of reality. Although some may be able to penetrate this fortress by having a good look, others require more training and cultivation (*bhāvanā*) which simply means that one is in need of mental integration and mental control.

Here we can recall the statement of the Buddha taken from the
old Pali Canons:
  Oh Brethren! Set an example (*caratha*) for the happiness and
  welfare of all sentient beings!
This passage is usually understood to mean: "Go ye Brethrens for
the happiness and welfare of all sentient beings!" However, the
text reads *caratha*, not *gacchatha*. *Cariyā* (Pali) which derives
from the verb-root *car* refers to how one goes about (*carati*) the
problems of life. The manner in which one goes about the problems of life leads to various forms of action. Of those, concentration is one. Concentration means to bring the mind under
control; not to allow it to turn loose and wild. There is also
the method which is known by the term meditation. Meditation is
considered to be a translation of the Sanskrit term *dhyāna*, but
according to the Tibetan tradition, *dhyāna* is considered to be a
kind of fixation. Certainly, in spite of the fact that it often
does, meditation is not meant to develop a fixation. There is
also the method of *samādhi* which is an active procedure of put-
ting things into their proper context from having seen things in
their proper way. Thus, it is on this *Path of Cultivation* that
one finds the *raison d'être* of the Eightfold Path. On the *Path
of Cultivation*, therefore, one is directed in his bodily actions,
proper speech, and mental integration through the stages of the
Eightfold Path.
  From this follows the final path, the *Path of No-more-learning*
(*aśaikṣa-marga*). The term *aśaikṣa* means: nothing more to learn.
Now this is a very tricky and misleading translation; however,
let me try to explain this term in the manner that the Buddhists
have interpreted it. If, for example, someone wishes to become
a surgeon, he must first study. It is also not enough that he
simply becomes a surgeon. He must be a good surgeon. Now
through his study, there comes a moment when he can perform
surgery. At this point, he no longer needs to look up his medi-
cal books and journals to find out where he is to insert the
scalpel into the body. He is so proficient that he can do this
automatically. This capacity to act without cogitation but
with the full confidence of knowing what must be done is like
the *Path of No-more-learning*. This path appears at the end of the
whole process of the five Buddhist Paths, but it is not an end as
such. This means that it is not a dead end. On the contrary,
it is an open-ended dimension which allows one to see ever new
facets. It is an infinite richness which defies to be captured
in the form of propositions. It is not, as some may surmise,
emptiness or voidness (*śūnyatā*).
  It is needless to say that the popular translation for this term
śūnyatā is "emptiness" or "voidness." However, it is one of
those strange Sanskrit terms of which, in an ordinary context, I
can make the statement, "*udakena śūnyaḥ*" when I wish to refer to

a container which has no water in it. As I have just mentioned,
I can make the statement *"udakena śūnyaḥ,"* but this statement
cannot be made when I wish to say something negative in an
ordinary sense. I must use some other collective terms such as
tuccha miccha to litigate that there is nothing. *Śūnya* is a
word which can be used without any qualifications, because it is
an utter fullness -- a fullness which is not contrasted with
emptiness or anything else. It has no limitation, because if it
had a limitation it would contradict itself. Thus, although the
texts inform us that this *Path of No-more-learning* is an open-
ended dimension (*śūnyatā*), it is not an emptiness or voidness
(*śūnyatā*). It has been referred to in the texts as Great Bliss
(*mahā-sukha*). In this moment, there are no disturbing, detract-
ing, or weakening forces. However, it would be wrong to say that
positive forces were acting, because the contrary views to which
we are so accustomed have lost their significance. So long as
contrary views -- the either/or -- are the founding substratum of
reality, we are literally groping in the dark. The logical-
constructs (*abhūta-parikalpita*) which is groundless and without
foundation is the constructing without a constructor. Herein
lies the paradox of the dynamic world in which we live. The
world of man, *ie.*, man's being-his-world, is an on-going open
dimension which when concretized by logical-construction looses
its magic. The rNying-ma-pas must be credited with their penetrating insight into reality which is an on-going flow
of "presencing" in which there never was anything (*med-bzhin
snang-ba*).
  In summary then, the Buddhist Path does not maintain a separation between man and the universe, nor does it reinforce our
dividedness against ourselves, which is the outcome of our
"having gone astray." Instead, it helps to heal self-inflicted
wounds by deeply involving us in the process of rediscovering the
identity of the forces operating in the observer and the observed world. While there is interplay of action and appreciation, both being experiences of a self-regulating and self-
transcending process, there is also, seen from another perspective, an interplay of man and his environment which is ultimately
designed to facilitate his "tuning in" to that wider reality
which he intuitively knows and feels to be his real home.

Levels of Language in Mystical Experience
By HAROLD G. COWARD

The method adopted in this paper is to begin by examining the
reports of practising mystics with regard to their experience
of language, and then to theoretically analyze the resulting
view of language. In reading the reports of practising mystics
it is soon evident that in mystical experience "language" is not
understood in any restricted or carefully defined sense. In
addition to the usual conception of language as the use of words
for the purpose of expression and communication, the mystics
think of language as including thoughts, gestures, events within
nature and even silence. Language, in all of these senses, is
experienced as having the power to discover or reveal meaning
within an individual's inner experience, in addition to the mun-
dane function of communicating meaning from person to person. In
mystical experience, it is the intra-personal revealing function
rather than the interpersonal communication function of language
that receives emphasis. Within the personal experiences of the
mystics, language functions in a variety of ways to reveal or
unveil the hidden meaning of reality.

I. LANGUAGE IN THE REPORTS OF MYSTICS

The power of words to uncover a deeper, more meaningful level
of experience is emphasized in the statement by Swami
Prabuddhananda. As he puts it, the inner personality has to be
soaked with spiritual (scriptural) words. Such words, when they
dominate one's speaking and thinking (thought here is simply
internalized speech), have the power to reveal truth and trans-
form character.[1] Because the word of scripture is experienced as
divine, the spiritual power inherent within can be maximized
when the word is repeated -- as in the chanting of a *mantra*.
Brother David Steindl-Rast also reports that the scriptural word
has spiritual power. In his practice this is seen most clearly
in the Jesus prayer -- chanting the name of Jesus synchronized
with one's breath and heartbeat.[2] For Rabbi Zalman Schachter
the practise of the Kabbalah requires immersion in the words of
the Torah and the hassidic masters so as to prepare the way for
the Divine influx into himself. In his experience it is in this
way that one "sets his own inner stage" and so opens the way for
the mystical experience.[3] Black Elk, the noted American Indian
mystic, reports that the words "Grandfather, Great Spirit, have
pity on me" are often continually repeated during his vision
quest practice.[4] However, for Eido Roshi, the Zen master, words

93

have a limiting function rather than a revealing power, and their
use is therefore to be avoided. As he puts it,[5]
"No dependence on words or letters;
Direct pointing at the Mind of Man;
Seeing into one's nature and the
attainment of Buddhahood."
In addition to the above familiar use of words in overt speech
or inner thought (internalized speaking), the mystics also suggest more esoteric conceptions of language, including "body
language" and "silence". Zalman Schachter notes that the "great
Zaddikim, like the Baal Shem Tov, are in touch not only with
heaven, but also grounded in their body, and even were known to
understand body-language and the language of plants and animals".[6]
In describing what he calls the holy carnality of his own practice
Rabbi Schachter says,
'From my flesh I see God'... When my body is in the right tone,
alive, aware and tingling, such vision becomes possible. I am
in touch with my vehicle and I can visualize the Divine, being
in touch with His name.[7]
In kabbalistic practice the words of the Torah and indeed God's
name itself is experienced as contiguous with one's body. The
body, therefore, is not only the temple of the spirit in which
God is known, but also a symbolic "language vehicle" for responding in praise.[8]
Although not so specifically stated, Brother David Steindl-
Rast's experience also evidences a mystical connection between body
aspects, divine spirit and language. He speaks of listening for
meaning with one's heart, for it is there that we are truly
"together".
Together with ourselves, not split up into intellect, will,
emotions, into mind and body. Together with all other creatures, for the heart is that realm where I am paradoxically
not only most intimately myself, but most intimately united
with all. Together with God, the source of life, the life of
my life, welling up in the heart. In order to listen with my
heart, I must return again and again to my heart through a
process of centering, through taking things to heart. Listening with my heart I will find meaning. For just as the eye
perceives light and the ear sound, the heart is the organ for
meaning.[9]
The Rule of St. Benedict, says Brother Steindl-Rast, is founded on
the practise of obedient listening to the inner word. " I must
give my ear, give myself, so fully to the word that reaches me
that it will send me ... by doing the truth lovingly, not by
analyzing it, will I begin to understand."[10] This means being
responsive to God's word in every person, every thing, every
event. And so God's word is in the eating of a tangerine, the
grasping of a friend's hand and even the experience of calamity.
94

The notion of language being immanent in all of creation is also found in descriptions of the Native American Indian's vision quest. In some isolated place such as upon a mountain, the seeker goes alone and sets out a sacred area within which he (i.e. the seeker) must remain in silence. Then one must listen carefully with intense concentration, for, as Professor Epes Brown puts it,

> ... it is believed that the sacred powers may manifest themselves through any form or being of the natural world, which may appear, visually, or which may wish to communicate through some audible message. The presence of the *word* of the Great Mystery is within every being, every thing, every event. Even the smallest being, a little ant for example, may appear, and communicate something of the power of the Great Mystery that is behind all the forms of creation. 11

The experience of the Native American mystics is that this "word" which is immanent in all of nature has a telos or "desire" to reveal itself to man. But only the person who through the purifying self sacrifice of fasting and exposure to the elements will be sufficiently humble and sensitive so as to be able to hear the surrounding voices that are speaking. Thus there is a great need for silence of both external action and inner thought so that the voice of the Great Mystery may be heard.

The need for a disciplined silence is also emphasized in the practice of Brother David Steindl-Rast. The purpose of the monastery is to provide an environment that helps one to learn to listen to the "word of God" that we find in all of nature and all of life's experiences. The monastic practice aims at detachment which decreases one's felt needs. Detachment is attained through the practice of silence. Brother David offers the following description, "Silence pervades monastic life in the same way in which noise pervades life elsewhere. Silence creates space around things, persons and events. Silence singles them out and allows us gratefully to consider them one by one in their uniqueness." 12 By such obedient listening the monk not only comes to hear the word of God in each event of life, but in thankful response, the monk himself literally becomes a manifestation of God's word. "In order to understand the word addressed to me, the word I am, I must speak the language of the One who calls."13 For Brother David this experience of the word provides a way of understanding the Christian mystery of the Trinity. "... the responsive listening in which my spiritual discipline consists is not dualistic communication. It is the celebration of triune communion: the Word, coming forth from Silence, leads by Understanding home into Silence."

The practice of Zen Buddhism by Eido Roshi also stresses silence, but here the unspoken implication with regard to language is different. Silence is required because words are conceptual constructions, and they serve either as spoken sounds or silent thoughts, to veil and distort the perception of reality. Language as uttered words or inner thoughts is the cognitive "noise" which obstructs the clear discriminating perception (*prajña*) for which the Zen mystic strives. Here the function of language is to negate itself and its necessary egocentricism, thus simultaneously purifying consciousness and revealing reality. This would seem to be the purpose of Zen meditation as practised by Eido Roshi.

Although the reports of the mystics evidence various emphases and valuations of language, it is clear that, for all, language plays an important function. It is also obvious that "language" is understood by the mystics in a very broad and fluid fashion -- encompassing the ordinary understanding of language as a means of inter-personal communication, but more often stressing the intra-personal revealing function of the Word immanent in scripture, gesture and all of nature itself. Disciplined silence is seen as the prerequisite practice for experiencing this intra-personal revelation. For the Hindu, Christian, Jewish and Native American mystics the silence sensitized the listener to the immanent Word. By contrast the Buddhist mystic practised silence so as to transcend the "noise" of conceptual forms and thus be enabled to directly perceive reality as it is in itself (*prajña*).

II.   IS THE MYSTIC EXPERIENCE OF LANGUAGE IRRATIONAL?

Since an analysis of the levels of language found in the reports of the mystics requires the placing of some confidence in those reports, and since some scholars may not be disposed to admit such confidence because the usage of the term "language" by the mystics is so fluid and all inclusive, let us first address the question, "Is the mystic experience of language irrational?" If a negative answer to this question can be reached, then perhaps there will be a more willing acceptance of the mystics statements about language as suitable evidence upon which to conduct further theoretical analysis.

In his recent and most helpful study of the methodology required for an academic study of mysticism, Frits Staal takes the following observation as his point of departure. The traditional Western prejudice is that mysticism in both its doctrines and experiences is *irrational* and, therefore, outside the scope of objective analysis.[14] This preconception of the irrationality of mysticism, which is held by many contemporary scholars, is often closely related to, if not couched in, the more general view that whereas religion is irrational, science is rational. The view that religion and, in particular, mysticism, is irrational is undoubtedly further strengthened (even if erroneously so) by the media's equating of such phenomena as

occult powers, seances, altered states of consciousness, and in
general any otherwise "mysterious" or unexplainable occurrence
with mysticism. Professor Principe clearly illustrated this
point in the opening lecture of this Conference.[15] Let us
assume, with Professor Principe, that mystical experience in its
classic forms is indeed something quite separate from the con-
fusing generalizations of the popular media -- and the reports
of the practising mystics, reviewed above, would certainly support
this view. The question then remains, "Is the experience of
language, reported by the mystics, irrational and therefore
outside the range of serious scholarly study?"

Although this question could occupy us at great length, it is in
this paper but a preliminary consideration and therefore must be
treated somewhat briefly. Fortunately Staal has investigated
this question at length and has arrived at the following con-
vincing conclusion.[16] Staal rejects the view that mysticism is
irrational and therefore cannot be rationally studied or understood. He argues that mystical experiences should be open to
rational analysis.[17] This statement he qualifies as follows:

To say that rational explanations can be given in these areas
does not imply that reason is our only, or even our best
faculty. I believe we can do better things than study. But
studying is a rational activity and if we decide to engage
in studying something then there is no point in the next moment in saying that it cannot be done because the domain is
irrational. The objects of our inquiry need of course not be
rational. Trees and rocks cannot meaningfully be called rational, but it does not follow that they are therefore unin-
telligible or cannot be studied rationally. 18

As a criterion for unintelligibility Staal puts forth the standard logical notion that if two contradictory statements about the
same thing are both presented as true, then inconsistency or
unintelligibility has been established.

Most objects, says Staal, are neither rational, nor irrational,
and yet can be the object of rational inquiry (e.g. plants,
which do not resist botanical analysis). Mysticism is such an
object, neither rational nor irrational in itself, but open to
rational study. To say this recognizes that the subject matter
of mysticism not only appears to be complex and often extraordinary, but also that countless contradictions will be encountered. But contradictions occur in virtually every realm of
study and are only an obstacle to rational enquiry when we
accept them as ultimate and give them explanatory value. Staal's
conclusion is that the search for rational explanation and
theories is, in the case of mysticism as elsewhere, meaningful,
fruitful and necessary.[19]

In the past, one point upon which the charges of irrationality
have focused is the high place given to intuition by mystics.

LANGUAGE IN MYSTICAL EXPERIENCE

At least two contemporary Western philosophers, Bertrand Russell[20] and F.S.C. Northrop[21] have denied that there is an opposition between the intuition the mystics advocate and the reason scientists demand. Both Russell and Northrop argue that intuition or insight is the initial experience which rational analysis subsequently confirms or denies. If this is seen to be acceptable for the heuristics of rational and scientific knowledge, then there is no reason why the inclusion of intuition in the reports of mystical experience should result in the judgment of irrationality being made. Of course careful rational analysis must follow upon the intuitive experiences if the study is to justify its claim to being rational in method.

A further obstacle which is sometimes raised to the rational study of mystical experience is that such experiences usually seem to be unique, rare, not easily repeatable, and perhaps not within the reach of everyone: hence, such experiences are not within the range of objective study. Staal points out that if such a line of argument were accepted then we would have to also exclude astronomy where experiences are often unique, the study of art since good artists are rare, and physics experiments such as the Michelson-Morley experiment which generated the theory of relativity. In all such cases the experiences involved are unique, rare, not easily repeatable, and require rigorous training in specific disciplines -- all of which conditions apply equally well to instances of mystical experience. Just as not everyone who trained to be a physicist and tried the Michelson-Morley experiments would succeed, or be invited to join the Princeton Institute for Advanced Studies, so also not everyone who tries Yoga, Kabbala, heyachastic practice or the vision quest will attain the goal, but that does not thereby imply that such experiences are irrational or do not exist.[22]

Taking into account all of these considerations, it appears that the mystical experience of language, which is a major component of the total mystical experience, is not by definition irrational. This does not establish that the mystical experience of language is rational. But it does show that the method of rational scholarship can be used to study the mystical experience of language. In the case of mystical language a rational approach would require the following steps. First, a sampling of mystical experiences of language. Since not all scholars have a mystical experience of language (just as not all doctors are afflicted with the rare disease they study) the first step is to become familiar with the phenomena in question by consulting with the persons who have had the experience themselves. In this study, it means coming to know of the experience of language through the reports of the mystics. This, of course, we have already done in the first section of this paper. This is the first step, namely, being sure that the scholars understand the reported experience in the same way as does the mystic. Of course, there will never be a perfect congruence between the scholars understanding and the mystic's experience, but the scholar must work very hard to get as close as the circumstances allow. In the end this means that he will have to engage in the mystic discipline himself, to begin with in a non-critical way, until he has sufficient "taste" of the mystical experience that he can empathize with and recognize the phenomenon that the mystic is reporting. To attempt to begin theorizing without first having seriously made this empathetic effort would be like a blind man busily working away on an analysis of sight. The second step is to step back from a trusting acceptance of the experience and to engage in critical analysis. The task of critical analysis requires the formulation of a theory which attempts to explain the phenomenon previously experienced. In the case of the mystical experience of language, some mystics from the Hindu tradition have themselves formulated such a theory. In the next section of this paper let us examine the formulations of Bhartṛhari, the 6th century Hindu grammarian, philosopher of language and saint, to see if his theory of "levels of language" seems a likely account for the reports of the mystics recounted in section one.

III. BHARTṚHARI'S "LEVELS OF LANGUAGE" INTERPRETATION OF MYSTICAL EXPERIENCE

Bhartṛhari is a renowned author in Sanskrit literature, philosophy and religion. Tradition says that we was a king who gave up his worldly life and became a holy man or *saṃnyāsin*. Recent scholarship dates Bhartṛhari ca. A.D. 450-500.[23] Bhartṛhari's theory of levels of language occurs in his *Vākyapadīya*, a treatise on grammar and the philosophy of language. The seventh century Chinese pilgrim to India, I-tsing, reports in his diary that in the education curriculum of the day Bhartṛhari's *Vākyapadīya*, coming after mastery of Patañjali's *Mahābhāsya* was the crowning work studied by the best and most serious students. Even in the great Buddhist university at Nālundā, the *Vākyapadīya* was studied alongside the eighteen schools of Buddhist philosophy.[24]

Bhartṛhari's thinking starts from the assumption that language must be taken as having existed beginninglessly; or, as somehow being coeternal with God. Here the viewpoint of Bhartṛhari seems very similar to the Platonic concept of the universality and eternity of the Idea. Whereas in Platonic doctrine the relation of the Idea to the "copies" is described as the relation of the immutable to its several manifestations, for Bhartṛhari the word (*sphoṭa*) is the immutable which is first perceived through its several physical manifestations. The word "cow", for example, is a word-form that is identical and immutable, although its physical manifestations may differ markedly with regard to accent, speed of speaking, place and time of utterance. But Bhartṛhari goes further than just establishing the eternality of language or word (*śabda*). He identifies it with Brahman -- all words ultimately mean the Supreme Brahman. Bhartṛhari bases this theory of language on the Vedic conception of *vāk* or speech. Speech (*vāk*) was considered to be a manifestation of the all-pervading Brahman, and the *praṇava* (*AUM*) regarded as the primordial speech-sound from which all forms of *vāk* have evolved. This sacred syllable is said to have flashed forth into the heart of Brahman, while he was absorbed in deep meditation, and to have given birth to the Vedas containing all knowledge. At the very beginning of the *Vākyapadīya* Bhartṛhari restates these very teachings as the foundation for his thinking.[25] Just as the original unitary Veda has been handed down in many ways by the *ṛṣis* for the sake of communication, so also the unitary word (*sphoṭa*) is manifested as a series of uttered sounds for the purposes of revelation, expression and communication.

For the *Vākyapadīya* the nature of the absolute eternal present is word (*śabda*) and consciousness (*caitanya*) inseparably mixed together, self-evident, and revealing of all knowledge.[26] This is *Śabdabrahman*. It is mainly due to the limiting function of time that *Śabdabrahman*, without suffering any loss, assumes differentiation as the intuited *sphoṭa* with its uttered words and manifested meaning.[27] At the lower levels of language, *vaikharī* (overt speech) and *madhyamā* (mental speech), the revealing power of the *sphoṭa* may be likened to a person looking at a landscape through a tube. The tube limits one's vision of the whole landscape, just as the forms of manifested language limit one's mental vision of *Śabdabrahman*.[28] However, the limited vision one does achieve by clear and concentrated looking is real -- but it is not the whole of the real. At the lower levels of language, with the limiting forms of spoken words and mental thoughts, repeated "looks" have to be taken at different "views" in an attempt to see the whole. At the upper, or *paśyantī*, level of language it is as if the tube has been taken away from the eye. The limiting forms of manifested speech (like the tube) have been transcended and the final omniscient vision is achieved. In terms of time the final *paśyantī* vision would be the eternal present in its wholeness. At the lower levels, the present would be the portion currently being "looked at"through the limiting forms, the past would be "views" previously seen, and the future, "views" yet to be seen. It is in this sense that Bhartṛhari conceives of the limiting function of time within language.[29]

When one is speaking, therefore, it is through the limiting power of time that the *paśyantī* level of word-consciousness assumes the lower and progressively more differentiated levels of *madhyamā* and *vaikharī*. From the hearer's point of view the process is reversed. The word-sounds (*vaikharī*) and the inner word-meanings (*madhyamā*) are both initially cognized under the sequence of time until, with the final perception of the whole (*vākya-sphoṭa*), the level of *paśyantī* is manifested. In this state of inner intuition noumenal knowledge dawns, and all differentiation due to the sequence of time is transcended.[30]

As we continue the description of Bhartṛhari's theory, let us now begin to refer back to the reports of the mystics to see if their experience of language fits with Bhartṛhari's theory. The first point noted in the reports of all the mystics, with the exception of Eido Roshi, was that words have power to uncover a deeper more meaningful level of experience. Swami Prabuddhananda, Brother David Steindl-Rast and Rabbi Zalman Schachter each engage in chanting or meditating on words, and usually the repeated words are scriptural. If we take the processes involved (and bracket or set aside for the moment the ultimate referent of the words which may well be different in each case, e.g. Brahman, Jesus and Yahweh), then the reports of the mystics seem to fit well with the explanation offered by Bhartṛhari. The repetition of words, especially scriptural words, has spiritual power for revelation of the divine through the process that Bhartṛhari has technically termed *sphoṭa pratibhā*. Concentrated study and repetition of the scriptural words progressively remove the ignorance or misperception clouding the mind of the devotee until the true referent of the word, the divine *sphoṭa*, is clearly seen. A helpful analogy describes how from a distance one (if one is in India) may mistake a tree for an elephant. But if one keeps on intensely looking at it, the tree is ultimately recognized in its true form. Similarly, in the case of the first exposure to a scriptural sentence or word, it may not evoke the highest language level of the divine referent (the *sphoṭa*), but instead be perceived as merely an uttered sound on the lowest or *vaikharī* level. However with concentrated study and constant repetition, the partial first level word-sounds (*dhvanis*) evoke a progressively sharper perception of the divine referent until finally it stands clearly revealed within one's consciousness (*sphoṭa pratibhā*). The psychological image behind Bhartṛhari's thinking is that by the process one's consciousness is purged of distractions or misconceptions which are preventing one from having a clear experience of the "divine consciousness" which is the ultimate reality within all beings. Brother David Steindl-Rast's thinking seems to fit closely with this theory when he talks of listening

101

to God's word as bringing us together with ourselves, together with other creatures and together with God, the source of life.[31]
Although the Zen Buddhist approach of Eido Roshi does not at all fit with Bhartṛhari's presuppositions as to the divine nature of language, the psychological process played by conceptual cognition on the middle or *madhyamā* level is seen by the two in very similar ways. For Eido Roshi language, as a man-made and therefore ego-attached conceptual construction, is an obstacle to the clear perception of reality (*prajñā*). In Bhartṛhari's theory too, the conventional forms of language are but partial verbalizations of the divine whole (the *sphoṭa*) and, thus, to the extent that the partial verbalizations of words and sentences are themselves taken to be ultimate conceptual forms, they act as an obstacle to the clear perception of reality (*Śabdabrahman*), e.g. elephant. Thus, for both, any fixation with, or dogmatic attachment to, conceptual forms at the middle level functions as a language obstacle to mystical experience and has to be overcome. (And as this Conference has evidenced, such an attachment to conceptual forms is the occupational hazard of academic scholars, and is quite probably the reason so few of us are mystics.) The definite difference between Eido Roshi and Bhartṛhari lies in their approaches to overcoming the obstacle of middle level conceptualizing. For Zen any further use of words would simply compound the problem, so silent meditation upon one's inflow and outflow of breath is the prescribed practice. However, for Bhartṛhari and the mystics who accept scripture, the conceptual forms of revealed words are held to be inspired language with the power to remove the obstructing or veiling function of ego-centred ordinary language. The situation is not unlike that of university teaching where the authoritative words of the professor are thought to help the student overcome his confused concepts and achieve a higher level of knowledge, i.e. the level of insight.
In the foregoing discussion it is clear that in mystical experience language may be seen to operate on at least two levels. On the one level there is *pratibhā*, or the intuitive flash-like understanding of the sentence-meaning or idea as a whole. In familiar terms it is the light-bulb-going-on in the cartoon situation. On the other level there are the uttered words of the sentence which try to communicate the unitary idea by breaking it down. Bhartṛhari calls the latter *vaikharī vāk* (overt or elaborated speech), while the former is aptly designated as *paśyantī vāk* (speech that through intuition, *pratibhā*, directly sees or perceives reality.)[32] Between these two levels, says Bhartṛhari, there is a middle or *madhyamā vāk* corresponding to the *vākya sphoṭa* or whole idea of the sentence broken down into partial meaning bearing units (words and phrases), none of which

have yet been uttered as word sounds. According to Bhartrhari these are the three levels of language through which speech or the word (*vāk* or *śabda*) passes whenever one speaks or listens. The word (*śabda*) which is at first quite internal, is gradually externalized for the purpose of communication. Or the student of mysticism may begin with merely the external series of what are at first the meaningless uttered letter sounds composing a *mantra* and then through concentrated study and repetition gradually internalize the sound until meaningful wholes are revealed (*sphoṭas*). The reports of all the mystics, with the exception of course of Eido Roshi, emphasized the importance of such a practice. In this way Bhartrhari accounts for all cognition as being necessarily identified with language, since these three levels of language span the complete continuum of cognition. This is clearly expressed in one of Bhartrhari's basic teachings. "There is no cognition in the world in which the word does not figure..."[33]

For Bhartrhari language is the essence of consciousness, and the means to all knowledge. And it must be clearly understood that by speech (*vāk*) or word (*śabda*) what is meant is the *conveyance or revelation of meaning*, and not the narrower but more usually understood reference to concept formation, the drawing of inferences, and so on, which would exist at the two lowest language levels (*vaikharī* and *madhyamā*) only. But when "meaning" is described as being intertwined with consciousness (as Bhartrhari maintains), this allows for instances of *pratibhā* (direct intuition) as well as instances of more commonplace cognition, and therefore can be held to be logically possible at all levels of *vāk* or speech -- from the cries of the animals to the most abstract of human words (e.g. as in the symbol *AUM*).[34]

It is just such a broad and inclusive theory of language that is required to explain the reports of the mystics presented in section one. Rabbi Zalman Schachter's reports of language as firmly grounded within the body are quite consistent with Bhartrhari's conception of language at the *vaikharī* level. Just as in kabbalistic practice the muscles, organs, and various parts of the body become the means for a material manifestation of God's word, so also for Bhartrhari, *vaikharī* is the most external and differentiated level in which language (*vāk*) coheres and functions. Included here are breath, mouth, gestures, ears, eyes, muscles, bones, nerves, and all the complex bodily functions involved in uttering and hearing sounds in a temporal sequence. *Prāṇa* or breath is taken to be the instrumental cause of language at the *vaikharī* or overt level, since it is breath that enables the organs of articulation and hearing to produce and perceive sounds in a temporal sequence. At this level the individual pecularities of the speaker (e.g. accent and style of speaking) are present along with the linguistically relevant

parts of speech. Earlier in the analysis it was noted that in
the experience of all the mystics the greatest obstacle to
spiritual attainment comes from the pride of ego attachment. At
the *vaikharī* or overt speech level ego attachment will be to such
things as one's vocal quality, accent, gestures and general
speaking ability. One of the psychological results of the
chanting of *mantras* in a disciplined fashion is the dropping off
of individual pecularities, the very stuff upon which ego attachment thrives, so that the timbre and tone of one's vocalizations
points to the divine referent rather than to one's self. Where
no divine referent is specified, and where word repetition is
not encouraged (as in Zen Buddhism), ego attachment to the style
of one's own vocalizations is effectively negated by the practice
of silent meditation.

Going further inward, as it were, to the middle level of
thought or mental speech (*madhyamā vāk*), we note a rich variety in
the reports of our mystics. For Swami Prabuddhananda, medita-[35]
tion is a constant flow of loving thoughts towards the Divine.
Brother David Steindl-Rast experiences himself as a word spoken
out of the Creator's heart and at the same time addressed by the
creator. "In order to understand the word addressed to me, the
word I am, I must speak the language of the One who calls."[36]
Such a description fits perfectly with Bhartṛhari's image of the
Divine word descending, expressing itself at the lower levels of
mental and overt speech, and then gathering back into itself in
the unity or, as Brother David puts it, the "intimate communion"
of *paśyantī*. In Bhartṛhari's view, it is the telos of language
both to burst forth into a differentia of expression (this is the
actual root meaning of Bhartṛhari's technical term *sphoṭa* --
"to burst forth") and then "to seek" out a return to the original
unity from which it began. The mystical experience of language
occurs when one identifies with the "return trip" movement of
this telos.

One characteristic of *madhyamā* level or mental speech in
mystical experience is the strong tendency toward symbolism.
This would fit with Bhartṛhari's finding that at the *madhyamā*
level the same idea (meaning-whole) or *sphoṭa* is capable of being
revealed by a variety of thought forms. It is in the kabbalistic practice of Rabbi Zalman Schachter that the symbolic
experience of language is highly developed. In Rabbi Schachter's
charts and explanations, the Hebrew words and letters of the
Torah are experienced as symbolizing and expressing the fundamental nature of the world and its relation to God. Symbolism
is also apparent in the report of Swami Prabuddhananda. He notes
that as the aspirant grows his conception of God expands from
the literal to the symbolic level. He moves from a small idea
of God to a larger and yet larger one until be sees God in
everything. This mystical experience is symbolized in different

ways. For example, he may consider himself and everyone else as sparks of the Divine; or, that he is connected with everyone and everything through the Divine, just as bubbles and waves are connected with one another through the ocean.

For both Brother David Steindl-Rast's Benedictine practice and Rufus Goodstriker's Native American tradition, the immanent divine word is experienced in symbolic ways. Meaning is encountered in the taste of a tangerine, the experience of calamity or in the activity of an ant within the sacred circle of the vision quest. In Bhartṛhari's theory such symbolism is the gateway to the highest level of language -- *paśyantī* or the direct experience of reality in its wholeness. At this level there is no distinction between thought and meaning, and there is no temporal sequence. All such phenomenal differentiations drop away with the intuition of the pure meaning itself. Yet there is present at the *paśyantī* level a "going-out" or divine desires for expression. This is the "instinct", "telos" or, to use a theological term, "grace" that may be said to motivate the phenomenalization of the unitary word into expression so that communication with those who are listening occurs. Thus in the words of scripture, the gesture of a friend's hand, the action of an ant or the ceaseless flow of a stream, the pure intuition of *paśyantī* becomes phenomenalized so that by its "uttered word" men might rise above their ignorance and be grasped in their cognition by the revelation of ultimate reality. Since the *paśyantī* or intuition level of language is, by definition, beyond the level of differentiated cognition, it is impossible to define it in word-sentences. It is at the level of direct intuition and therefore must finally be understood through experience.

To conclude let me summarize the ground we have covered. In this paper it has been argued that the mystic's experience of language although broad and flexible in nature, need not necessarily be branded as *irrational*. In examining the evidence (i.e., the reports of the practising mystics with regard to their experience of language) it was found that for many, although not all of the reports, Bhartṛhari's language theory proved to be a helpful theoretical explanation of the levels of language in mystical experience.

NOTES AND REFERENCES

1 See statement by Swami Prabuddhananda "Spiritual Disciplines of a Practising Mystic According to Hinduism", p 23

2 See statement by Brother David Steindl-Rast, p 21

3 See statement by Zalman Schachter "The Humanistic Transcendentalist Practice of the Kabbalah", p 31-32

4 As reported by Joseph Epes Brown "The Question of 'Mysticism' within Native American Tradtions", p 115

5 A personal communication.

6 Zalman Schachter, *op. cit.*, p 32

7 *Ibid.*

8 *Ibid.*, p 33

9 Brother David Steindl-Rast, *op. cit.*, p 19

10 *Ibid.*, p 20

11 Joseph Epes Brown "The Question of 'Mysticism' Within Native American Traditions", p 114

12 Brother David Steindl-Rast, *op. cit.*, p 21

13 *Ibid.*, p 22

14 Frits Staal *Exploring Mysticism* (London: Penguin Books, 1975 pp 27-59

15 Walter H. Principe "Mysticism", pp 1-2

16 *Exploring Mysticism op. cit.* Pt. I. Although I agree with Staal's argument regarding the possibility of a rational approach to the subject matter of mysticism, I object to his move to separate mysticism from religion. This seems to be part of his desire to dissociate mystical experience from what he calls the "irrationalism of Christianity" (see pp 29-39) . In his view it is this Christian irrationalism which is the root cause of the contemporary Western prejudice that mysticism is irrational (p 27). It seems to me that this desire to separate mysticism from religion runs the danger of reductionism of reducing it to something less than it itself claims to be. (See for example, the unity of religion and mysticism in the reports of our practising mystics.)

17 *Ibid.*, p 67

18 *Ibid.*, pp 13-14

19 *Ibid.*, p 16

20 Bertrand Russell *Mysticism and Logic* (London: Allen & Unwin, 1959) p 18

21 F.S.C. Northrop *The Logic of the Sciences and the Humanities* (New York: Macmillan, 1947)

22 Staal, *op. cit.*, pp 57-58

23 H.G. Coward *Bhartṛhari* (Boston: Twayne, 1976) p 12

24 As reported in *The History and Culture of the Indian People The Classical Age* ed. by R.C. Majumdar (Bombay: Bharatiya Vicya Bhavan, 1962) pp 586-89

25 *Vākyapadīya of Bhartṛhari*, trans. by K.A. Subramania Iyer (Poona: Deccan College, 1965) I:5-10

26 *Ibid.*, I:123

27 *Ibid.*, I:3

28 *Ibid.*, I:142

29 See *vṛtti* on *Vākyapadīya* I:142

30 For a more detailed discussion see Chapter Two of my *Bhartṛhari* (Boston: Twayne, 1976)

31 Brother David Steindl-Rast, *op. cit.*, p 19

32 *Vākyapadīya*, *op. cit.*, I:142

33 *Ibid.*, I:123

34 *Vākyapadīya* II:145-152. The Translation of Chapter II of the *Vākyapadīya* has been provided by K. Raghavan Pillai (Delhi: Motilal Banarsidass, 1971)

35 Swami Prabuddhananda, p 24

36 Brother David Steindl-Rast, p 22

The Question of "Mysticism"
within
Native American Traditions
By JOSEPH EPES BROWN

Contemporary uses of the term "mysticism" and its cognates have
come to apply to a wide variety of often disparate phenomena, fre-
quently far removed from the early Christian or original Greek
sense of the terms. It may indeed be said that the term has become so often abused, and levels of reality so confused, that in
certain contemporary contexts "mysticism" may actually express the
inverse of, or the grossest parody on, those great mysteries and
mystics of the legitimate and orthodox great religious traditions
of the world.

Examples of abuse and misuse could be cited from a plethora of
modern cults, "the new religions," popular parodies on legitimate spiritual or mystical ways, not to mention experimentations
with instant "mystical experiences" afforded through the agencies
of various drugs. A number of such expressions have been well
pointed to by Professor Coward in his initial background statement for this conference. To underline, however, at least certain dimensions of such problems one may recall the statement of
Aldous Huxley in *The Doors of Perception*, written in 1954:

> It has always seemed to me possible that, through hypnosis, for
> example, or auto-hypnosis, by means of systematic meditation, or
> else by taking the appropriate drug, I might so change my ordi-
> nary mode of consciousness as to be able to know, from the in-
> side, what the visionary, the medium, even the mystic were
> talking about.[1]

That contemporary confusions concerning the prerequisite conditions for true spiritual realization abound in the world today is
eminently comprehensible and evident to many. Under the forces of
a pervasive materialistic outlook, spreading essentially from the
Western world, and causally related to the erosion of the great
spiritual legacies of this world, man has become increasingly a
prisoner of the limits of his vision and the manner in which he
experiences his world. In seeking release from this constricting
experience of a continually changing physical multiplicity, and
motivated by a nostalgia for a lost more real world of true freedom, many have turned in every possible direction for alternate
answers. Due, however, to the erosion and spiritual impoverish-
ment of one's own proper tradition, or rather, due to man's
inability in these times to understand the true nature of these
traditions, there is left no real criteria for discrimination,
evaluation, and eventual choice rooted in true knowledge. In

addition, there is the problem that motivation in the quest, often undertaken with the greatest sincerity, may actually be, through the self-will of the ego, sentimentality, or the desire, self defeating in itself, for some other-worldly, liberating mystical experience which nevertheless still appears within the realm of limiting phenomena. Under such conditions there is no guarantee that what is found will not lead to further frustrations, and often, as is the case with altered states of consciousness through the use of drugs, to a sinking within the lower chaotic depth of one's being, and thus to a deepening intensification of the original problem.

One response to this dilemma, which has already been implied above, may perhaps best be phrased through the following question: is it still possible, given the force of contemporary circumstances, for man to re-establish his broken links with one of the great world religious traditions, that is, with one of those particular and providential expressions of what has been called the *philosophia perennis,* that perennial and timeless wisdom valid nowever and forever? That such may be the only way has been affirmed by an increasing number of scholars of the sacred such as Ananda Coomaraswamy, René Guenon, Seyyed Hossein Nasr, or the great contemporary European theologian and metaphysician, Frithjof Schuon, who has unequivocally stated that:

...there is no possible spiritual way outside of the great orthodox traditional ways. A meditation or concentration practised at random and outside of tradition will be inoperative, and even dangerous in more than one respect; the illusion of progress in the absence of real criteria is certainly not the least of these dangers.[2]

It is suggested that these general introductory considerations are particularly relevant to the discussion to follow on Native American religions, and specifically on the nature of "mysticism" as expressed and experienced within the context of these spiritual traditions.

It has, first of all, long been necessary to situate correctly the so-called "primitive religions" within the context of the world's historical religions, and in so doing to recognize, or at least that is the hope, that in spite of many elements unfamiliar to the outsider, these Native traditions, at least where there has not been excessive compromise to the modern world, are in no sense inferior, but indeed are legitimate expressions of that same universal *philosophia perennis*. The injustices suffered by these world-views, ritual practices, and life-ways, through ignorance and ill-will, through deeply rooted prejudices and wilfull falsifications, all commencing with the first European contacts with the "new world," now demand that a reevaluation take place and that proper recognition and respect be given. There

are indeed signs today that such positive reassessment is taking
place, and what is especially encouraging is the extending realization on the part of many Native Americans themselves, who had
lost or neglected their proper religious traditions, that such
traditions and related life-ways do constitute within the world
of today not only a viable reality in themselves, but also a valid
and powerful response, in terms of fundamental values, to many of
the problems faced by the contemporary world. That there is a
progressive strengthening of this realization is nothing short of
miraculous when one considers those pressures for abandoning
these traditions, in the name of "progress" and "civilization,"
which have been exercised against the people over the past
centuries.

One explanation for the current new willingness to understand
Native Americans and their life-ways is the fact that, being
rooted in this american land for thousands of years, the Indians'
otherwise very diverse cultures have all come to express rich
spiritual relationships with this american land; indeed the forms
and symbols bearing these values are all drawn from the details of
each peoples' particular geographic environment. Native Americans
lived, and many still do live, what one might call a metaphysic
of nature, spelled out by each group in great detail, and defining
responsibilities and the true nature of that vast web of man's
cyclical interrelationships with the elements, the earth, and all
that lives upon this land. They are the echoes of such a message
that above all have caught the attention of at least a few within
a society that finally has been forced by hard circumstances to
recognize the gravity of our ecological crisis, and thus to seek
answers that speak to root causes rather than continually treating
the ever recurring symptoms of the problem.

Many of the younger generations especially, who formerly had
turned to distant lands and seemingly exotic traditions for answers to the problems of our world, have now come to see in expressions of Native American wisdom a more meaningful message, because these sacred traditions, as has been expressed above, are
rooted in, and take their expressions from, elements of this very
land with which many today, in their sense of alienation, seek
meaningful relationships. Further, many individuals discern a
deep mystical element in these sacred traditions of the Indian,
and it is within something of this vision that they themselves
would participate.

The problems, however, for the outsider who would personally
relate to the sacred vision and practices of the American Indian
are just as critical as, or even more problematic than, the attempt to relate to any of the orthodox traditions of East or West.
The problem essentially lies in the tendency for the individual
not rooted in any tradition to use an alien and thus often exotic
religious tradition as a screen upon which to project all that one

seeks yet finds lacking in one's own world. Rarely is the prerequisite effort made to understand the alien tradition on its
own terms, through the categories of its proper language, and thus
for what it really is in all its profundity and complexity, and
with its impelling sacrificial demands. One is too easily satisfied merely to "touch the earth," to nourish one's own personal
sentiment and nostalgia, and to hope thereby that somehow some
mystic vision of ultimate meaning will automatically and easily
come through.

Against the background of the above considerations, it is now
possible to speak more directly to the theme of this conference,
and to ask the following question: If "mysticism," in its original and thus deepest sense, is an experiential reality within
Native American spiritual traditions, what are the conditions under which such experience becomes operative, and what are some of
the contours of its manifestations? To answer this difficult
question with any degree of justice, and within the necessarily
brief space allowed, it is suggested that certain illustrative
examples be drawn from the peoples and traditions of the Plains
and Prairies because the place of this Conference is within this
vast geographic and native culture area, and also because the major living and academic experiences of this present author have
been with the peoples and religious traditions of the Plains,
specifically with the Lakotas, the Assinoboine, the Crow, and the
Blackfeet. It should initially be stressed that obviously there
are rich differences across the cultures of the diverse Plains
peoples, and yet at the same time, and particularly at the level
which especially concerns us here, there is also a homogeneity of
means and spiritual experience which allows generalizations within
certain limits.

The essential thesis which it is intended to develop in that
which follows is that "mysticism," insofar as it is a reality within these native traditions, is not, as the outsider has tended to
view it, a vague quality of some supernatural experience which
spontaneously comes to individuals whom providence has allowed to
live close to nature. Rather, attempt will be made to demonstrate
that such "mystical" experiences are first of all prepared for,
and conditioned by, life-long participation in a particular spoken language which bears sacred power through its vocabulary,
structure, and categories of thought, and which serves as a vehicle for a large body of orally transmitted traditions, all
the themes of which also express elements of the sacred. Second-
ly, such "mystic" experiences become more available to those persons who have participated with intensity and sincerity in a
large number of exacting rites and ceremonies which have been revealed through time, and which derive ultimately from a transcendent source. There are also, through the nature of the peoples'
life-ways rooted in hunting activities, interrelationships, in-

112

formed by the rich oral traditions, with all the animal beings
and the forms and forces of the natural environment. Further,
there comes into plan the supporting exposure to a rich heritage
of art forms, both visual and audible, many of which are repre-
sentations of a supernatural experience received by the executor
of the form. One may also mention the support offered by the
dynamic rhythm of continually living out the myriad details of an
everyday life, all the forms and acts of which are enriched by
the inherent dimensions of the sacred. All these elements, and
more, provide a specific, all-encompassing, supporting frame within which each individual lives out his or her life. It is essentially through the conditioning support and force of such spiritual forms and orientations that the individual becomes open to
the possibility of receiving through dream or true vision,
glimpses of sacred realities born perhaps by the forms of the
Natural world, yet more real and permanent than the fleeting relative reality of this immediate world. The force of such traditions is so pervasive that it is understandable why it was expect-
ed that every man and woman should in solitude and with suffering
participate in the so-called vision quest, or should seek a
"guardian spirit," not only at the time of puberty, but indeed
continuing regularly throughout their lives. A vision or guardian
spirit helper may not always come to every seeker, but there is
much evidence that such experiences did come to many of the people
with great frequency. The fact, incidentally, that among many of
the groups outside of the Plains the vision quest tended to be the
exclusive province of the shaman, has led Robert Lowie and others
to refer to the Plains experience by the intelligible, yet somewhat unhappy term--"democratized shamanism."

It is necessary to the clarification of our thesis to define in
greater detail not the specific and often ritual requirements of
the formalized vision quest, which time will not allow, but rather
to speak of what one might call the spiritual contours and implications of the quest. In such necessarily condensed treatment
one is impressed by the remarkable parallels to be found with
expressions of the historical religions, and which have been so
beautifully expressed by the statements of our colleagues in this
Conference. Not that such parallels suggest borrowings, but
rather one may say that where the hearts and souls of men are exposed to the powers inherent to legitimate sacred traditions,
there appears a common quality of spiritual realization which
transcends cultural differentiations.

In Plains cultures no person should seek the vision experience
without the help of a wise spiritual guide, an older person who
has experienced visions and who has received special powers
through guardian spirit helpers. Only such a person is aware of
the dangers facing the seeker, and only he will be able to interpret for the novice that which might come to him or her in either

an intense dream or a vision. Interpretation is important, for it
is believed that the nature of the experience received indicates
the directions and qualities a person's life should take. In the
case of an especially strong experience the recipient will be in-
structed to secure some particular form or being from the natural
world, and this will become part of a "medicine bundle," which
will continue to actualize the particular power or quality received. Many of the sacred symbolic and often abstract paintings,
such as those found on shields, represent such concrete represen-
tations of the supernatural experience, and these thus insure
continuity of the power inherent to the experience throughout the
person's life.

The vision quest must always be preceded by rites of purification through the use of the sweat lodge. Here the novice is
helped to enter into the necessary state of humility, to undergo,
as it were, a spiritual rebirth. The person also, through rites
and prayers, and through the form and materials of the lodge itself, is aided in establishing relationships with the primary elements, earth, air, fire, and water, and with all the beings of the
earth, the animals, the winged creatures, and all that grows from
the earth. Such relationships are additionally strengthened in
these rites of purification through the use of a sacred pipe, the
communal and sacramental smoking of which establishes a ritual
relationship with all of creation and with the very source of life.

The quest itself must be undertaken in solitude and in silence
upon a mountain, or some isolated place well away from the camp.
The seeker's state of concentration is aided through the delin-
eation of a protecting sacred area within which the person must
remain and move about only in accord with a prescribed ritual
pattern, usually defined by the four directions of space in their
relation to an established center. One must always be attentive
and listen, for it is believed that the sacred powers may manifest themselves through any form or being of the natural world,
which may appear visually, or which may wish to communicate
through some audible message. The presence and word of the Great
Mystery is within every being, every thing, every event. Even the
smallest being, a little ant for example, may appear, and communicate something of the power of the Great Mystery that is behind all forms of creation. The powers and beings of the world
wish to communicate with man; they wish to establish a relationship, but may only do so where the recipient is in a state of
humility, and is attentive with all his being. Since such humility is fostered through sacrifice, the seeker must neither eat
nor drink for the duration of his quest, often three or four days.
Being there alone and almost naked, he will realize the force of
the elements through exposure and suffering. It has been said by
many that the greatest support in the quest, and in the course of
life itself, is silence, for ultimately silence is the very voice

of the Great Mystery. The man or woman, however, is also enjoined to pray, indeed to pray continually, either silently, in an audible voice, or through song. The old Lakota sage, Black Elk, once told the writer of a prayer he often repeated continually during his quests. It was simply: "Grandfather, Great Spirit, have pity on me." In prayer, he also said, one should express thankfulness, gratitude, for all those gifts which are upon and above this earth.

Throughout that sacred lore given in sincerity and generosity to the outside world by many Plains peoples, there is ample evidence that through their sacred traditions and ritual practices, true mystical experiences in intense dream or vision did come to many seekers, and indeed they became such an accepted reality within these cultures that it was believed that no man or woman could ever be anybody, or could ever be successful in any undertaking important to the peoples' lives, unless one had received the spiritual power of the mystical vision experience. It is also true, as must always be the case, that some did not receive. Such persons, nevertheless, could participate in something of the power of the experience of others, even though less directly, due to the frequent obligation on those who received to express their experiences, as has been mentioned earlier, in concrete manner through paintings, song, or sacred forms of dance.

It should be added that mystical experiences did not come to the people exclusively through the actual vision quest, for often such experiences came through participation in other rites and ceremonies such as those of purification, through participation in the great annual sacrificial Sun Dance, or due simply to the general conditioning powers and sacred content of the totality of their traditions, men occasionally did receive such experiences at any time in their daily lives. Good evidence of this is found, for example, in the life of an exceptional man such as the Lakota, Black Elk. It may also be said of such a man that his frequent experiences, and the weight of their message and requirements, placed an enormous burden upon him, causing intense suffering throughout his entire life.

It may also be added at this point that mystical experiences such as the vision, which after all does appear in some phenomenal form, need not be a necessary criterion for, or a proof of, a true and integrated spiritual realization. The experience may simply provide probably evidence that the recipient has achieved at least a certain state of realization. Many traditions, it should be recalled, view visions, and mystical experiences generally, with suspicion, and suggest that such could provide dangerous distractions to a true spiritual way.

If at this point the question be raised as to what criteria can be used to affirm the spiritual authenticity of religious traditions such as those of the Native Americans, and the reality of mystical experiences to which such traditions give rise, at

least one response, if one may be so bold as to walk such dangerous ground, might be as follows:

The tradition in question must have its origins in a sacred
source which is transcendent to the limits of the phenomenal
world. All the expressions and extensions of this tradition will
then bear the imprint of the sacred, manifested in terms appropriate to the time, place, and condition of man. In relation to
man's active participation, the tradition will provide the means,
essentially through sacred rites, for contact with, and ultimately a return to, the transcendent Principle, Origin, or by whatever name or term this be called. True and integrated progress
on such an inner journey demands the means for accomplishing the
progressive yet accumulative integration of the following elements or spiritual dimensions: 1) *Purification*, understood in a
total sense, that is, of all that man is, of body, soul and
spirit; 2) *Spiritual Expansion*, by which man realizes his totality, his relationship to all that is, and thus his integration
with, and realization of, the realm of the virtues; 3) *Identity*,
or final realization of unity, a state of oneness with the ultimate Principle of all that is. Spiritual expansion is impossible without the prerequisite purification, and ultimate identity is impossible outside of the realm of virtue, wholeness, or
spiritual expansion.

These themes of purification, expansion, and identity, however
they may be termed, are inherent, it is suggested, to all the
true spiritual ways of the orthodox and thus legitimate traditions of the world. In regard to the situation of the Native
American Traditions, it is hoped that sufficient evidence has
been provided to demonstrate that these traditions, where they are
still relatively intact, do not lie outside of such criteria, but
rather, in accord with their primordial origins, they represent
legitimate spiritual dialects of that *philosophia perennis* already referred to.

The dominant question raised in this presentation concerned
those individuals who seek for a way which will provide answers
to the multiple problems posed by the crises and spiritual pov-
erty of the contemporary world. In terms of answers being found
within Native American spiritual traditions, it was suggested
that in spite of the initial attractiveness of these traditions,
because they are rooted in this land, and because of their seem-
ing "mystical" qualities, such traditions are nevertheless generally inaccessible to the non-Native American for reasons which
one trusts have been made clear through the discussions in this
paper. What is a possibility, however, is that by taking the
pains to learn what one can from Native traditions, one who as yet
is affiliated with no true tradition, will be aided in knowing
what *a* tradition is in all its complexity, depth, and richness of
cultural expressions. This being understood, it is then possible

to undertake the work of rediscovering the roots of what normally, or historically, should be one's own spiritual heritage, and
now seeing and commiting oneself to that heritage with the new
vision that distance and perspective often allows. This is a
way which demands sacrifice, as all spiritual ways do in any case,
but it is now a way that is not an escape, but has that integrity
and rigor which must always provide hope.

FOOTNOTES

1 Aldous Huxley *The Doors of Perception* (London: Chatto &
   Windus 1954)
2 Frithjof Schuon *"Des stations de la Sagesse"* Franc-Asie
   No. 85-86 Saigon,1953. Pp 507-513.

 SUPPLEMENTS

---

1. FOOTNOTES TO A THEOLOGY
The Karl Barth Colloquium of 1972

Edited and with an Introduction by
MARTIN RUMSCHEIDT

1974   149 pp.
ISBN 0-919812-02-3 $3.50 (paper)

2. MARTIN HEIDEGGER'S PHILOSOPHY OF RELIGION
JOHN R. WILLIAMS

ISBN 0-919812-03-1 $4.00 (paper)

3. MYSTICS AND SCHOLARS
The Calgary Conference on Mysticism 1976

Edited by
HAROLD COWARD
and
TERENCE PENELHUM

ISBN 0-919812-04-X $4.00 (paper)

Available from:

WILFRID LAURIER UNIVERSITY PRESS
Wilfrid Laurier University
Waterloo, Ontario, Canada N2L 3C5

EDITIONS

1. LA LANGUE DE YA'UDI

Description et classement de l'ancien parler de Zencirli dans le cadre des langues sémitiques du nord-ouest

PAUL EUGENE DION, O.P.

1974   509 pp.
ISBN 0-919812-01-5 $4.50 (paper)

STUDIES IN RELIGION / SCIENCES RELIGIEUSES
Revue canadienne / A Canadian Journal

Abonnements / Subscriptions

Abonnement personnel: $10.00 (quatre fascicules)
Abonnement pour les institutions: $15.00 (quatre fascicules)
Fascicule isolé : $4.00

Individual subscriptions: $10.00 (four issues)
Institutional subscriptions: $15.00 (four issues)
Individual issues: $4.00

ISSN 0008-4298

Tout chèque doit être fait à l'ordre de Wilfrid Laurier University Press.
Make cheques payable to Wilfrid Laurier University Press

WILFRID LAURIER UNIVERSITY PRESS
Wilfrid Laurier University
Waterloo, Ontario, Canada N2L 3C5